ESSAYS ON THE STUDY OF URBAN POLITICS

ESSAYS ON THE STUDY OF URBAN POLITICS

Edited by
KEN YOUNG

Foreword by
Edward C. Banfield

ARCHON BOOKS
1975

© *The Macmillan Press Ltd 1975*

First published 1975 by
THE MACMILLAN PRESS LTD
*London and Basingstoke
and in the United States of America
as an Archon Book, an imprint of*
THE SHOE STRING PRESS, INC.,
Hamden, Connecticut 06514

Printed in Great Britain

Library of Congress Cataloging in Publication Data

Young, Kenneth George.
Essays on the study of urban politics.

Includes bibliographical references and index.
1. Municipal government — Addresses, essays,
lectures. 2. Metropolitan government — Addresses, essays, lectures. I. Title.

JS91.Y68 1975   320.4'173'2   74-30040

ISBN 0-208-01400-4

Contents

Foreword

In the past two decades political scientists on both sides of the Atlantic have given increased attention to urban politics. In part this has been a response to the growing demand for 'solutions' to social problems that seem, and in some instances are, unprecedented in nature and critical in importance. But in the main it has reflected the aspiration of a new generation of scholars to vindicate the claim implicit in the words 'political science' by producing a systematic and cumulative knowledge about behaviour in the political arena closest to hand.

No one will say that these efforts have had much success. To be sure, the practical people who struggle with the problems of the cities nowadays turn more often to political scientists for information and advice. It is not cynical, however, to suggest that they may do so because it is politically expedient to invoke academic auspices. (In the singular, the term auspice means 'omen drawn from birds', and in the plural form means 'protection extended' or 'patronage'.) Nor is it unfair to remark that the information and advice that the practitioners have received from the political scientists has seldom helped them very much in coping with city problems.

But this is not what is most discouraging. If the political scientist could point to a small but powerful set of theoretical tools he might well shrug off any complaints that the practical people might make. 'All in due time,' he might say. 'We have here the beginnings from which knowledge will grow at an exponential rate. Before long there will be a fund of it more than adequate to your needs.' Unfortunately, however, there does not exist such a set of tools. Despite the thousands — tens of thousands more likely — of articles and books in which concepts have been explicated, models constructed, hypotheses framed and data reported and analysed, there are not half a dozen general and non-trivial scientific propositions which an urban political scientist can offer to the waiting world. Admittedly, he is hardly any worse off than his fellow social scientists, but this is rather cold comfort.[1]

What is wrong? How does it happen that after so much effort by so many people in so many places (much of it *serious* effort by intelligent people) we have so little of practical or scientific interest to say about political behaviour in urban settings?

There are, I think, three great difficulties in the way of an urban political science. Although not peculiar to the subject matter all are more or less inherent in it.

Firstly (and no importance is to be attached to the order of the listing), the urban political scientist cannot satisfactorily specify the object he is investigating. What do we mean by 'urban' political phenomena? Is urbanism a habitat, a state of mind, the outcome of an interaction between the two, or something else? And what exactly are its features or traits? (Here the political scientist may find comfort in the knowledge that other social scientists confront the same difficulty. The sociologist Paul Wheatley concludes after an elaborate review of the literature on urbanism, that 'it is impossible to say more than that it is compounded of a series of sets of ideal-type social, political, economic and other institutions which have combined in different ways in different cultures and at different times', and that 'it is not unlikely that the only feature which such congeries of institutions will ultimately prove to have in common is the fact of their aggregation.[2]) Can one use such a slippery and ill-formed concept as an independent variable in order to predict how people will vote, whether they will suffer from alienation, or how much and what sort of conflict will be

---

[1]   If anyone has doubts about this he has only to look through the 600-odd pages of Bernard Berelson and Gary A. Steiner (editors) *Human behaviour, an inventory of scientific findings* (New York: Harcourt Brace Jovanovich, 1964).

[2]   In Peter J. Ucko, Ruth Tringham and G. W. Dimbleby (editors) *Man, settlement, and urbanism* (London: Duckworth, 1972).

engendered by their living together? Similarly, can one treat
the concept as the dependent variable and proceed to say
how it is affected by styles of leadership, governmental
structure or patterns of conflict?

One does not improve matters much by substituting the
concept 'city' for the concept 'urban'. As Williams remarks in
his essay in this volume, 'all that takes place in cities is not
necessarily urban'. The city cannot generally be taken as the
unit of investigation because there are regional and other
interdependencies some of which give rise to integrative
efforts — a matter which Young explores in some detail —
and because there are wide differences of interest and of
opinion and also in power not only between public and
private bodies but also among a wide variety of types of each
— a matter illumined by Lewis' account of lay-professional
relationships in the provision of social services. Ironically
(Stanyer's essay seems to support this inference) the more
precisely we identify the object of investigation, the less we
are able to say about what in ordinary language is called
urban politics.

Secondly, the urban political scientist, because he studies a
rag-bag of matters, is obliged to employ a rag-bag of concepts
and theories. Most of these are borrowed and they come
from very diverse sources: economics, sociology, psychology,
communications theory, organisation theory, cybernetics . . .
Consequently we find urban political behaviour being 'explained' by patterns of land use, the structure of labour
markets, class culture, ethnicity, neighbourhood identification, and what-not. With one hand, so to say, the urban
political scientist holds his odd assortment of tools while
with the other he grasps distinctively political institutions,
practices and modes of thought. This requires a good deal of
dexterity, as all of the contributors to this volume demonstrate in one way or another. Elkins' applications of organisation theory provide a particularly good example.

Thirdly, the urban political scientist cannot settle upon a
'one best way' of doing empirical research. The nature of his
subject matter requires him to get the 'feel' of a concrete
political system or sub-system, and this necessitates a case-
study method: nothing can take the place of close observa-

tion of a very small universe in getting this kind of understanding. If the 'feel' does not set the imagination working so
as to produce systematic theory (the consummation devoutly
to be wished, of course), it is nevertheless useful in other
ways, as by sensitising the researcher to such differences
between concrete settings as render a theory that is applicable to one inapplicable to the other. Newton exemplifies
this by pointing to the pitfalls in applying methodology of
American community power-structure studies to the quite
different British case.

I hasten to add that no amount of case material can suffice
adequately to test scientific hypotheses. One need not share
Davies' strong confidence in what can be achieved by statistical model-building in order to acknowledge this. But it must
also be said that model-building is not enough either. The
most extensive data and the best constructed model are
valuable only in so far as the concepts that guide the selection and interpretation of data are appropriate. And from
whence do appropriate concepts come? In the last analysis
from the commonsense of one who has a 'feel' for the concrete situation. In short, there is no way for the model
builder to get his feet altogether out of the clay of mere
hunch and guesswork and on to the high ground of scientific
rigour.

To these three obstacles in the way of an urban political
science which are inherent in the nature of the field I must
add a fourth for which we have only ourselves to blame. This
is that our studies do not build one upon another: they do
not add up to a body of knowledge. Of course, everyone
agrees about the need for replication. There are, however,
very few studies that are truly replicative. Replication is dull
work; it is much more fun to strike out in some direction of
one's own. Besides reputations are made in the profession by
being (or seeming to be) 'original', not for doing again what
someone has already done. It is not surprising, then, that we
have many tracks but very few paths.

The essays in this book all reflect in some degree and in
one way or another what I have maintained are the difficulties inherent in our subject matter. For me their chief
interest lies in the variety and ingenuity of the authors'

efforts to face up to these difficulties. The book presents a collective challenge to all who aspire to carry the study of urban politics forward — a challenge that (I dare say) the authors join me in hoping will quickly be accepted.

EDWARD C. BANFIELD

Preface

This volume of essays is offered as a modest celebration of three recent developments in the field of urban politics. In the first place, it is intended to mark the growth in inter-actions between scholars from both sides of the Atlantic. Until the late 1960s, such intellectual traffic as existed was sporadic in nature and recognisably unilateral. Today, British students of urban politics are increasing their contacts with their American counterparts, while urban affairs in Britain and Continental Europe have become an additional concern of North American researchers. These reciprocal contacts are reflected in the activities of the European Consortium for Political Research, for example, or in the Anglo-American Round Table on Urban Politics held at the University of Essex in 1973. These essays have arisen from the new dialogue, long may it continue to flourish.

Secondly, these essays mark the maturation of British urban political science. For many years the field (itself in-distinguishable from 'local government studies') was domin-ated by legal-historical-descriptive accounts of structures of government. Such accounts were often written in a strongly critical and reformist tone, a feature which rarely makes for convincing analysis. Today, studies of that type, although still in evidence, have been relegated to their proper place as mere adjuncts to explanatory studies; for this we must pay tribute to Jim Sharpe of Nuffield College, Oxford, who played the leading role in the reorientation of British local government studies. The young British political scientist in the 1970s knows his Dahl, his Hunter, his Bachrach and Baratz. Let us hope that we will resist the natural temptation to mistake erudition for scholarship, and so avoid merely re-placing the institutional anecdote with the uncritical citation from 'the literature'.

Thirdly, these essays celebrate the establishment and early days of *Policy and Politics*, a journal to which the readers of this volume will need no introduction. Originally conceived as a special issue of the journal, this collection subsequently expanded to the point where separate publication became preferable. All the contributors who appear here have been involved in *Policy and Politics:* Davies as the scholarly and authoritative editor; myself as his junior partner; Banfield as our kindly and encouraging American adviser; Stanyer and Newton as hard-working members of our editorial board; Williams and Elkin as stimulating contributors; Janet Lewis as a catalyst in the journal's foundation and subsequent abstracts editor.

But the celebratory aspect of these essays is of course secondary to their substantive purpose. I began by asking the original contributors to delineate the separate areas within the field, and to review their state of development. Each chapter was to serve both as milestone (this is how far we have travelled) and as signpost (these are the directions in which we may proceed). The overall collection was intended to achieve a clearer prospect of the field of urban political inquiry, to demonstrate the relationship between its several aspects, and to point up alternative avenues of exploration. Behind this aim lay my hope that both the marginal colleague and the intending student would be able to take this book from the shelf in order to see what we are about. These essays are consequently addressed to those audiences as much as to the mainstream urban political scientist.

The tolerant reader will not expect these somewhat exacting standards to have been fully met. Nor have all the approaches been uniform, for my role as editor has been to let the authors speak for themselves rather than force consistency upon them. As a result, some authors adopted a predominantly rear-view mirror perspective upon their part of the field. Others have proved more strongly oriented to future developments, and have taken the opportunity to set out original analyses.

The collection is organised in the following manner. Kenneth Newton begins with a review of issues in the American community power studies and their lessons for

British research; his essay is also intended to be read by those American scholars planning to carry out fieldwork here. This review is followed by Jeffrey Stanyer's discussion of the state of urban electoral analysis, in which a model of urban elections is set out. Next come two essays which reflect the current interest in the determinants of urban service provision and the necessary complementarity of research techniques: in the first, Janet Lewis argues for the recognition of a wide range of causally significant and often elusive variables; in the second, Bleddyn Davies sets out an approach to handling some of these variables through multivariate analysis. Oliver Williams follows with an argument for the centrality of the spatial dimension in urban political analysis. Next comes my own essay on the political integration of metropolitan areas, which draws upon international theory. Stephen Elkin extends the range of analysis with a discussion of the pitfalls of cross-national urban inquiry.

The seven essays are intended to be read as a single set with some degree of thematic continuity. But there are limits to the degree to which such continuity can be achieved without forcing, and for this reason I take up some of the points raised by contributors as well as a number of more general considerations in the final chapter.

Canterbury   KEN YOUNG
June 1974

Notes on the Contributors

EDWARD C. BANFIELD is William R. Kenan Prôfessor of Government in the University of Pennsylvania; he was previously Professor of Urban Government at Harvard University, and has also taught at the University of Chicago, where he received his doctorate in 1952. Edward Banfield is the author of numerous articles and nine books on urban politics, planning, and related subjects, including *Political Influence* (1961), *Big City Politics* (1965) and the controversial *The Unheavenly City* (1970).

BLEDDYN DAVIES is currently Director of the Personal Social Services Research Unit at the University of Kent at Canterbury and joint editor (with Ken Young) of *Policy and Politics*. He read Economics at Cambridge and obtained his doctorate at Oxford. He taught at the University College of Wales, Aberystwyth, before joining the teaching staff of the London School of Economics in 1963. He is the author of seven books and a number of articles on variations in local authority policy outcomes, including the pioneering *Social Needs and Resources in Local Services* (1968).

STEPHEN L. ELKIN is presently Acting Director of the Masters of Public Administration Program and Assistant Professor of Political Science at the University of Pennsylvania. He formerly taught at Smith College and was a Fellow of the Joint Centre for Urban Studies, Harvard — M.I.T. Stephen Elkin received his doctorate from Harvard University in 1969; his *Politics and Land Use Planning: The London Experience* was published in 1974.

JANET LEWIS obtained a first degree from Edinburgh University and a Diploma in Social Administration from the London School of Economics. This was followed by two years as a family case worker with Family Service Units. She then spent three years at the Guy's Hospital Medical School on research into local authority health visitors before beginning the research reported here at Goldsmiths' College, London. Janet Lewis is currently research fellow at the Centre for Studies in Social Policy, London, where she is studying community representation in the reorganised National Health Service.

KENNETH NEWTON came to the study of urban politics via studies in sociology at the Universities of Exeter and Cambridge and through a course in political sociology which he taught at the University of Birmingham. His interest in comparative urban research took him as visiting professor to the University of Pittsburgh in 1972 and to the University of Wisconsin, Madison, in 1973-4. He has conducted extensive research into the political life of Birmingham and has written a number of articles or urban politics as well as *The Sociology of British Communism*. Kenneth Newton is now research fellow at Nuffield College, Oxford.

JEFFREY STANYER studied at Balliol College, Oxford, where he obtained his first degree and a B.Phil. in Politics. He joined Exeter University as research fellow in local government in 1960, and since 1962 has been lecturer in politics there. He has held two research grants from the Social Science Research Council for the study of local electoral behaviour and has written a number of articles as well as contributions to the symposia *Voting in Cities, Local Government in England 1958-69,* and *The Role of Commissions in Policy-Making.* He is the author of *County Government in England and Wales* (1967).

OLIVER P. WILLIAMS is currently Professor of Political Science at the University of Pennsylvania, and was formerly chairman of the Department of Political Science. He obtained his first degree from Reed College, and his master's degree and doctorate from the University of Chicago. Apart from a number of articles, Oliver Williams is co-author of *Four Cities* (1963) and *Suburban Differences and Metropolitan Policies* (1965). His *Metropolitan Political Analysis* was published in 1971.

KEN YOUNG obtained his bachelor's and master's degrees and his doctorate at the London School of Economics. He was for two years with the Greater London Group there, left to teach in the Sociology Department at Goldsmiths' College, London, and returned to L.S.E. as research officer in the Department of Government in 1969. Since 1974 he has been research fellow at the University of Kent at Canterbury, and joint editor (with Bleddyn Davies) of *Policy and Politics*. A contributor to *The New Government of London* and *By-Elections in British Politics,* Ken Young has a book in press on the Conservative Party in local government and is preparing a new political history of metropolitan London.

Community Politics and Decision-Making: The American Experience and its Lessons*

Kenneth Newton

The systematic study of community politics and decision-making started in the United States, and Americans have produced such a gigantic quantity of literature that it seems only sensible to start here when thinking of the directions that British research might take. We can learn from American mistakes, avoid red herrings and blind alleys, and perhaps learn a few short-cuts. At the same time, one cannot simply transplant research approaches from one country to another without allowing for important national differences. The lessons of the American experience must be carefully adapted to suit the British context, and to do this we must know something about the ways in which the American research has developed.

THE AMERICAN EXPERIENCE

A rich seam of research work was laid down in the 1920s and 1930s in the United States, but for present purposes the modern study of urban politics and decision-making started in 1953 with the publication of Floyd Hunter's *Community Power Structure,* a study of Atlanta, Georgia.[1] On the face of

*I am pleased to express my thanks to the American Council of Learned Societies for a Research Fellowship which enabled me to spend a year with the Department of Sociology at the University of Wisconsin, Madison. The paper was written while I was at Madison.

[1]   The quantity of published work in the community power and decision-making field is so enormous that it would be impossible to give even a selected list of the most important works in this short piece. However, a complete bibliography will appear shortly: see Irving P. Leif and Terry N. Clark, 'Community Power and Decision-Making', *Current Sociology,* forthcoming. For an extremely useful collection of readings, together with some original work and a bibliography, see Michael Aiken and Paul E. Mott (eds.), *The Structure of Community Power* (New York: Random House, 1970).

it Hunter's method was as simple as it was ingenious, for he simply selected a number of well-placed informants who were believed to have a full and reliable knowledge of local politics, and asked them to name and rank the influential people in the city. The people named most frequently were considered members of Atlanta's power structure. Because this method is relatively quick and cheap, and because it can claim to provide inside information about local politics which could otherwise be collected only after many years of participant observation, the method was taken up by a large number of community power researchers. It became known as the reputational method, and although it was elaborated and refined in many different ways, the basic approach remained the same — to find well-informed respondents who could draw up lists of influential people. Like many of those who used the reputational method after him, Hunter found an elitist power structure in Atlanta in which about forty leaders, most of them businessmen, set the framework and content of public policy. These few crowds or cliques of businessmen, Hunter concluded, used the machinery of city government to ensure that decisions were made in their own interests.

Hunter's methods and conclusions were quick to draw fire, and there followed a long and often acrimonious debate which continues up to the present time. It was said that the reputational method is no more than a complicated way of asking local inside-dopesters for a quick rundown on the local big shots, an approach often used by newspapermen with just about the same validity and reliability of results. The main criticism was that the reputational method is appropriately named because it never gets beyond reputational or perceived power to real or actual power. Informants may know what is really going on, but they may not. They may base their opinions on idle gossip or the gospel truth, but there is no way of distinguishing gospellers from gossipers. Consequently the method may pick out the powerful but it may pick out those with nothing more than a reputation for power, and while it is true that what people do is affected by what they believe others have the power to do — the rule of anticipated reactions — the relationship between reputed power and actual power has never been examined at all closely.

There is also some ambiguity about the central terms 'power' and 'influence'. It is argued that Hunter confuses the potential to do things, based on control of resources like money or political office, with actually doing them, as shown in political activity which influences the course of events. One man may have great potential for power, but not use it; another may have little potential but exploit it to the full. There is also the strong possibility that the informants may use the terms 'power' and 'influence' in a variety of different ways. Social scientists themselves find difficulty with closely related terms like 'power', 'influence', 'control' and 'authority', so there is no reason to believe that laymen, intelligent or otherwise, will use the words in any consistent way. It is all too easy to confuse power with status and, as a result, the reputational method may not pick out the most powerful, but simply the most visible and conspicuous.[2] Lastly, there are problems about the scope of power. A man may be powerful in educational matters but relatively powerless on housing issues, so it may be misleading or entirely meaningless to produce general power rankings over all issue areas in the community, as the reputationalists tended to do.

It is also claimed that the reputational method produces self-fulfilling prophecies. Just to ask the question 'Who is powerful?' is to assume that some people are powerful and others are not, and the term 'power structure' implies a more or less stable pattern of power relations, as compared with a more fluid and impermanent pattern.[3] Moreover, Hunter picks out the forty names mentioned most frequently by his

---

[2]   A reputational sort of question in Glossop uncovered the name of a community leader who had died thirty years before: A. H. Birch, *Small Town Politics* (London: Oxford Univ. Press, 1959) pp. 41-2. Another British study found that a reputational-type question about power in the community had little meaning for members of the city council: J. Blondel and R. Hall, 'Conflict, Decision-Making, and the Perceptions of Local Councillors', *Political Studies*, Oct 1967, p. 344.

[3]   Some people, the present writer included, do not use the term in this way, and suggest that power structures may range from rigid, elitist ones all the way to fluid, amorphous and rapidly changing ones.

informants, and then points to the small size of the elite. But why pick out forty? Why not four hundred, or four thousand, or just four? In addition, Hunter never really shows that the top forty operated as a more or less cohesive elite, something he must do if he is to demonstrate his case for the existence of a single power elite in the city.

In short, the reputationalists have been accused of assuming the answers to the questions they set out to investigate, of asking leading questions, of working with self-fulfilling prophecies, of using intolerably sloppy methods and concepts, and of systematically ignoring evidence they did not like. The obvious response to this onslaught is to verify the reputational results against the results yielded by other methods, something which quite a few people have tried to do, although with differing results. But this tactic makes little sense. The great strength of the reputational method is also its great weakness — its claim to give the inside story which cannot be uncovered in any other way short of years of participant observation. The need for an inside story will be felt as long as there are social scientists who believe that politics is a dirty game and that we can see only half of what goes on. According to this view of politics, some of the most important decisions may be taken in secret sessions held behind locked doors in smoke-filled rooms full of wheeler-dealer politicians who threaten and bluff and bribe and bargain as well as stab each other in the back and sell each other down the river.[4] The only way of getting reliable evidence about this hidden part of the decision-making process is for the social scientist himself to become involved, either as a participant observer or as an influential politician. Since neither strategies are possible in most cases, and since both have their own drawback in producing hard evidence, the investigator has to rely on indirect information produced by people who he hopes are reliable. But the reputationalist is at the mercy of his informants. There is no way of checking their evidence against that produced by more 'objective' methods.

[4]   This was written in the year of Watergate, the Vice-Presidential resignation, and several more minor scandals in British politics.

Dissatisfied with reputational methods and elitist conclusions, a second school of community power studies
developed, starting with the publication of work by Edward
Banfield and Robert Dahl in 1961, and later developed by
Nelson Polsby, Raymond Wolfinger, Aron Wildavsky and a
host of other writers. Instead of studying reputations for
power, the work attempted to get a picture of real power by
analysing actual decisions. By using interviews, newspaper
reports, official documents and participant observation, the
aim was to reconstruct key political decisions in order to see
who initiated them, who opposed them, and who won and
lost the political battle. The decision-making method, though
more expensive and time-consuming than the reputational
method, seemed to have the advantage not only of sorting
out those with real power (if, indeed, there were such
people), but also of showing the ways in which they exercised their power. Besides using a different method, Dahl and
Banfield and those who followed after them uncovered
different sorts of power relations in their communities.
Instead of finding elitist power structures they found pluralist ones in which power was generally distributed between
different groups and individuals depending on the issue, the
time and the place. Dahl wrote: 'I would contend that in
most American communities there isn't a single "centre" of
power. There is even a sense in which *nobody* runs the
community. In fact, perhaps this is the most distressing discovery of all: typically the community is run by many
different people, in many different ways, and at many
different times.'[5]

The next round in the debate picked out some of the
difficulties with the decision-making method and the conclusions associated with it. In the first place, there are problems with the selection of 'key issues'. Dahl himself admits to
a degree of arbitrariness in choosing issues,[6] and there may
also be a tendency to pick out the more dramatic and public

[5]   Robert A. Dahl, 'Equality and Power in American Society', in W.
      V. D'Antonio and H. J. Ehrlich (eds.), *Power and Democracy in
      America* (Notre Dame, Ind.: Univ. of Notre Dame Press, 1961) p.
      75.
[6]   Ibid. pp. 104-5.

issues rather than more routine matters, even though the latter may be cumulatively more important. There is also some evidence that the more dramatic and visible issues tend to generate pluralist types of power relations, whereas the great majority of more routine ones may be associated with different sorts of power structures.[7] There may even be a certain circularity in the decision-making method in so far as it involves picking out salient public issues, and since these issues are contested by different sides they have, almost by definition, a strong pluralist element in them. Moreover, by selecting and reconstructing current political battles, there is a tendency to overlook the funnel of causality set up by past decisions and outcomes, many of which set up a whole series of constraints on present action.

Those who use the decision-making method are also prone to overlook certain possibilities by virtue of the way in which they define power. If power is the ability to get one's own way despite the resistance of others, then an operational test for power is to see whose will prevail's in a conflict situation. The problem arises with what Bachrach and Baratz call the second face of power, which involves not making a decision against a background of conflict, but making a non-decision by preventing the issue from ever reaching the public arena in the first place. Bachrach and Baratz quote Schattsneider's point that while some issues are organised into politics others are organised out.[8] Community power studies, therefore, should concern themselves not only with those who influence decisions, as the pluralists have done, but also with the

[7]   Some evidence for this assertion is presented in K. Newton, 'Pluralist Theory and the Participation of Voluntary Organisations in Community Politics', paper presented to the Annual Meeting of the American Sociological Association, New York, 27-30 Aug 1973. For a general discussion of the way in which different types of decisions may be associated with different types of power relations, see Theodore J. Lowi, 'American Business and Public Policy, Case Studies, and Political Theory', *World Politics*, Sep 1964, pp. 701-16.

[8]   Peter Bachrach and Morton Baratz, 'Decisions and Nondecisions: An Analytical Framework', *American Political Science Review*, Sep 1963, pp. 632-42, and 'Two Faces of Power', *American Political Science Review*, Dec 1962, pp. 947-52.

possibility that some may be powerful enough to decide (*a*) what issues are to go on to the public agenda and (*b*) the ground rules for deciding these issues, and (*c*) the further possibility that some groups may not act on an issue because they fear the likely reactions of the powerful members of the community. The whole non-decision-making argument is only a short step away from the suggestion that a community may contain groups which are powerful enough to manipulate public opinion and create a false consciousness among some sections of the public.

This 'neo-elitist' argument was quickly countered by the pluralists who claimed that non-decisions are non-events, and non-events cannot be empirically investigated in any direct fashion, if they can be investigated at all. There are also severe philosophical problems with the concepts of false consensus and false consciousness. How does one tell if a consensus is false or genuine? As a result, some writers would like the whole discussion of non-decisions and false consciousness banned from the realms of empirical social science. However, this argument is rather like saying that things which cannot be measured do not exist, and besides, there is too much empirical evidence that some forms of political apathy and inaction are caused by feelings of powerlessness to be able to dismiss the non-decision-making argument out of hand. More recently a serious attempt to study non-decision-making in a systematic and empirical manner has been published and, while the work is open to some lines of criticism, it has pushed the debate forward on both the theoretical and the empirical front and pointed the way to future research strategies.[9]

In the same way that the decision-making method directs attention towards decisions and away from non-decisions, the method also focuses attention on the organised rather than the unorganised. Any given issue may well involve conflicting groups, each trying to protect and expand its interests, but what about those sections of society which are unable to

[9]   Matthew Crenson, *The Un-Politics of Air Pollution: A Study of Non-Decision-making in the Cities* (Baltimore: Johns Hopkins Press, 1971).

participate in the group battle simply because they are poorly organised or totally unorganised? Research shows clearly enough that middle- and upper-class people are often members of a wide range of organisations, but that working-class people are often without these affiliations and, to this extent, may be severely handicapped in the pluralist struggle.[10]

For all these reasons the pluralist position is less strong than it seemed at first, and the debate between pluralists and elitists, or neo-elitists, goes on. By and large, sociologists have chosen the reputational method and there is a tendency for this method to yield elitist conclusions. Political scientists have leaned rather more to the decision method and are more likely to reach pluralist conclusions. What makes the debate between the two sides rather curious is the fact that their empirical conclusions are often not too dissimilar. Most studies find relatively low levels of public participation in community politics and most find that a fairly small number of people are continuously active, most find a high proportion of middle- and upper-class people among the activists, and most find that decision-makers are generally unencumbered by any direct influence exerted by the mass of citizens, although indirect influence may be exerted by different groups in different ways. What seems to distinguish elitists from pluralists as much as anything else is not so much their findings as the different ideological frameworks within which they present and interpret them. Hunter is highly critical of politics in Atlanta and evidently believes that the city falls far short of the democratic ideal. His introduction states that his concern for the future of democracy prompted his study. Dahl is much less critical of New Haven politics and believes that it is not too remote from a reasonable notion of practical democracy. He says that over-optimism about democratic possibilities in large-scale industrial society will only breed cynicism and that, while New Haven certainly does not achieve a textbook perfection, it is a good example of what a real (pluralistic or polyarchical) democracy looks like, warts and all. The difference appears

10   Michael Parenti, 'Power and Pluralism: The View from the Bottom', *Journal of Politics*, Aug 1970, pp. 501-30.

to lie as much in what the two hoped to find as in what they actually found. Hunter seems to have set his sights higher than Dahl and is disappointed. To put words into their mouths, Dahl might say that Hunter is unrealistic; Hunter might suggest that Dahl is complacent.

Besides reaching conclusions that were not entirely dissimilar, the early elitist and pluralist studies were alike in two further respects: they were based on case studies of single cities, and they asked the question 'Who governs?' without asking what difference it makes to the community. Later work tried to go beyond the limitations of case studies by comparing a small number of communities, but it soon became clear that it was difficult to generalise on the basis of four, five or six cases. The next step was to collect together the large number of case studies and rework and classify the material. In this way, data from as many as 166 studies could be reused.[11] Although this produced some interesting and useful results, it also proved difficult to fit a number of individual case studies into a single comparative framework, so the next wave of research started to collect comparable data in a systematic manner from a number of cities.[12]

As well as shifting into a fully fledged comparative stage, the work also broadened the range of questions it asked about community politics. Instead of asking 'Who governs?', the questions now became 'Who governs, where, when and with what effects?'[13] The focus of attention broadened from

[11]   Claire Gilbert, *Community Power Structure* (Gainesville: Univ. of Florida Press, 1972); M. Aiken, 'The Distribution of Community Power: The Structural Bases and Social Consequences', and John Walton, 'A Systematic Survey of Community Power Research', both in Aiken and Mott (eds.), *The Structure of Community Power*; Terry N. Clark *et al.*, 'Discipline, Method, Community Structure, and Decision-Making', *American Sociologist*, Aug 1968, pp.

[12]   See the variety of reports which appear in Terry N. Clark (ed.), *Community Structure and Decision-making: Comparative Analyses* (San Francisco: Chandler, 1968); Peter H. Rossi and Robert L. Crain, 'The NORC Permanent Community Sample', *Public Opinion Quarterly*, Summer 1968, pp.261-72.

[13]   Terry N. Clark, 'Power and Community Structure: Who Governs, Where and When?', *Sociological Quarterly*, Summer 1967, pp. 291-316. This article is reprinted in Charles M. Bonjean, Terry N. Clark and Robert L. Lineberry (eds.), *Community Politics* (New York: Free Press, 1970), along with many other valuable pieces.

a study of power structures to the relationships between power structures, community characteristics and policy outputs. Under community characteristics were included a range of social and political variables such as class and ethnic composition, industrial structure, region, city size and age, political culture, and type of city government. Policy outputs included a whole range of particular decisions such as fluoridation, urban renewal and school desegregation, as well as more general studies of budgeting and expenditure patterns.[14] The interest in urban public policy developed so rapidly that it became an activity in its own right and deserves separate treatment from this account of community politics and decision-making studies. However, it can be mentioned that a study of public policy can make an important contribution to an understanding of power relations in a community, in so far as groups which benefit may be thought of as more powerful than groups which do not.[15] Meanwhile the older tradition of community power studies continues apparently unaffected by the more recent developments in the field.[16]

[14]   Robert L. Crain, Elihu Katz and Donald B. Rosenthal, *The Politics of Community Conflict: The Fluoridation Decision* (Indianapolis: Bobbs-Merrill, 1968); Peter H. Rossi and Robert A Dentler, *The Politics of Urban Renewal* (New York: Free Press, 1961); Michael Aiken and Robert R. Alford, 'Community Structure and Innovation: The Case of Public Housing', *American Political Science Review*, Sep 1970, pp. 000-000; Robert L. Crain, *The Politics of School Desegregation* (Chicago: Aldine, 1968); Robert L. Lineberry and Ira Sharkansky, *Urban Politics and Public Policy* (New York: Harper Row, 1971); Terry N. Clark, 'Money and Cities', mimeo.

[15]   See M. David and Paul E. Peterson (eds.), 'Introduction', *Urban Politics and Public Policy* (New York: Praeger, 1973); Edward C. Hayes, *Power Structure and the Urban Crisis: Who Rules in Oakland?* (New York: McGraw-Hill, 1972).

[16]   For recent work, see Edward O. Laumann and Franz Urban Pappi, 'New Directions in the Study of Community Elites', *American Sociological Review*, Apr 1973, pp. 212-30; James M. Williamson, 'The Ecological Approach to Measuring Community Power Concentration: An Analysis of Hawley's MPO Ratio', *American Sociological Review*, Apr 1973, pp. 230-42, and the letters by Hawley and Williamson in the following issue; Delbert C. Miller, 'Design Strategies for Comparative International Studies of Community Power', *Social Forces*, Mar 1973, pp. 261-74.

SOME LESSONS FOR BRITISH RESEARCH

Hidden away in the huge mass of American work there are some important lessons for English research. In the first place, it is clear that community power studies have had their day, at least in the form worked out by Hunter and Dahl. Experience has shown that answers to the 'Who governs?' question are both more simple and more complex than the original work presumed, and that the question has to be broken down and reformulated. In the second place, the question has much less relevance to Britain than to America. Cities in the United States are enormously diverse in terms of their class, ethnic, religious and industrial composition, their regional cultures, and their age and historical experience. They also have a wide variety of formal local government structures: there are weak and strong mayor/council cities, council/manager cities, and a handful of metropolitan governments and commission cities. Some cities use referenda extensively and others do not, some have local election primaries and others do not, some have at-large elections while others have ward-based elections, some have non-partisan elections in fact, others only in theory, and some have no party restrictions at all. Some cities have broad and independent powers conferred upon them by their charters, and others 'cannot operate a peanut stand at the city zoo without first getting the state legislature to pass an enabling law'.[17]

Perhaps most important of all, local government in the United States is fragmented. It is divided geographically into municipalities, counties and townships, and functionally into sanitation boards, pollution control boards, education boards, water districts, school districts and housing authorities. The New York Metropolitan Region is governed by 1,400 separate political entities, and the six counties which make up the Chicago metropolitan conurbation contain very nearly one thousand separate local government units, each with the power to tax. Altogether there are some 80,000 units of local government in the United States. Some

[17] Edward C. Banfield and James Q. Wilson, *City Politics* (New York: Random House, 1963) p. 65.

of these units are further fragmented by virtue of the separation of executive and legislative branches of government, and by virtue of the fact that some public officials, such as police and fire chiefs, have their own basis for political power. In some cases the different pieces of the mosaic cut across each other so that the various local government agencies compete and openly conflict with each other for power and resources. In this sort of situation the 'Who governs?' question is acutely problematical.

The situation in Britain is very different indeed. National parties operate in each city on the basis of nationally understood policies, even though the policies may vary to some extent from one locality to another. The mass media are much more highly centralised than is the case in the United States, and the country has a more homogeneous political culture with an ethnically more homogeneous population. And although few students of British local government would call the system a model of rational organisation, it is nevertheless a great deal more unified and centralised than its American counterpart. Cities are very similar in terms of their formal government structure and in terms of their relationships with central government, and the whole system is relatively highly centralised and unified at both local and national levels. The result is that the 'Who governs?' question is far less problematical in the British context, at least in the initial stages of research. One simply starts with the elected and appointed officials of the local authority and works from there. The trail may lead to Whitehall and Westminster, or to local party organisations and pressure groups, or it may turn to council committees and group officers, or to any combination of these. The point is that one can sensibly forgo the preliminary stages which are necessary in the vast majority of American cities, and save much time and trouble into the bargain.

This line of reasoning is not based on speculation alone. Two empirical studies demonstrate the irrelevance of American community power methods to British cities. A study of Bristol used the reputational method, only to find that the council was the centre of local decision-making.[18] It would

---

[18]   Delbert C. Miller, *International Community Power Structures* (Bloomington: Indiana Univ. Press, 1970).

have saved much time and trouble to use what is already known about British local politics by starting with the council as the centre of decision-making. A second study, conducted by someone who understood the British context, did start from this point and, after analysing seventeen local issues, shows the extent to which the formal office-holders on the council dominated the decision-making process of the city.[19] In their own ways, both studies show that it is both theoretically and empirically justifiable to make initial assumptions about where community decisions are made (if not about who makes them or brings pressure to bear on them), thereby avoiding many of the methodological and practical problems of American research.

A second major lesson in the American research, dealt with by Elkin elsewhere in this volume, is the crucial importance of seeing local politics in its national framework and of analysing the interplay of national and local factors.[20] If it is wrong for American scholars to make city-state assumptions, then it is clearly completely beyond the pale for British scholars to do so. In fact, one of the most important research needs is to explore the relations between central and local government policy. One possible way of approaching this is to draw a distinction between policy-making, policy application, and policy uptake. As far as policy-making is concerned, a major problem is the extent to which local government policy is made by central government, local government, or a mixture of both. We have to understand the ways in which local authorities, either singly or collectively, through community pressure groups, political parties or professional associations, are able to influence or even determine central government policy.[21] If some central government policies are determined by local pressures, then they are not centrally

[19] B. S. R. Green, 'Community Decision-Making in Georgian City', Ph.D dissertation (Bath Univ. of Technology, 1967).

[20] For a theoretical and empirical discussion, see Theresa Brown, M. J. C. Vile and M. F. Whitemore, 'Community Studies and Decision-Taking', *British Journal of Political Science*, Apr 1972, pp. 133-53.

[21] For two studies of this kind, see Brenda Swann, 'Local Initiative and Central Control: The Insulin Decision', *Policy and Politics*, Sep 1972, pp. 55-63; and Howard Scarrow, 'Policy Pressures by British Local Government', *Comparative Politics*, Oct 1971, pp. 1-28.

made at all.[22] On the other side of the coin, local authorities may cut their policy proposals to fit central government views on the subject. It is difficult to believe that a Labour council would present a serious comprehensive education plan to a Conservative government without first checking on the probable reaction. Policy-making on any given issue is likely to show both central and local government influences, and both levels are likely to frame proposals in the light of the anticipated reaction of the other, but the operations are inadequately understood at present.

The policy application side of the process may be even more complicated.[23] While central government has a wide choice of formal and informal mechanisms for seeing that its policies are applied, local authorities also have their tactics and strategies for doing what they want. Central government itself may consciously apply policy differentially in different places and at different times, perhaps because the policy was laid down by a preceding government or because the policy is not having the intended effects and needs modifying in practice. Nor do local authorities necessarily observe central government policy with the same degree of exactness: some may abide by the spirit of the policy, some by the letter, some may bend the policy, others break it, and others may look for loopholes. Reactions to the recent school milk and rent rise issues suggest that local authorities may choose all sorts of different means to achieve the same ends, and all sorts of different means to achieve different ends. One important research exercise would be to examine the application of central government policy at the local level, to see how different authorities respond to the same stimuli.[24]

---

[22] See James Fesler, 'Approaches to the Understanding of Decentralisation', *Journal of Politics*, Aug 1965, pp. 536-66.

[23] For a general discussion of policy application, see Thomas B. Smith, 'The Policy Implementation Process', *Policy Sciences*, June 1973, pp. 197-209, and the same author's 'Policy Roles: An Analysis of Policy Formulators and Policy Implementors', *Policy Sciences*, Sep 1973, pp. 297-307.

[24] See, for example, E. M. Sigsworth and R. K. Wilkinson, 'Constraints on the Uptake of Improvement Grants', *Policy and Politics*, Dec 1972, pp. 131-41.

There may also be wide variations in the way in which street-level bureaucrats interpret and apply policy directives. Local government officers are often subject to role-conflict, depending upon the demands of politically determined policy and the demands of their professional norms. The interplay may cause either greater or smaller variations in policy application, depending on whether national professional standards are stronger than allegiance to local policy-makers.

Lastly, different areas and populations may respond in different ways to the services created by local government policy. Some may take up services with alacrity and others may be slow off the mark. It has often been observed that services intended for the poor have been grasped by the more affluent, one example being the use of improvement grants made by middle-class people to modernise their second homes bought in improvement areas. However, we have scarcely begun the serious and systematic study of the variations in policy uptake so far as this is affected by, and has its effects on, local politics and policy-making.

The preceding comments have hinted at one theme which is noticeably lacking in the American literature and is dealt with at length elsewhere in this volume — the possibly crucial role of bureaucrats in local decision-making. The literature rarely draws any clear distinctions between elected representatives (politicians) and appointed officials (bureaucrats), partly because there is not the same tradition of a large, professional, bureaucratic apparatus, but partly from research oversight. Whatever the cause, British research must clearly take account of the possible influence of central and local government officers on local politics and decision-making.

While it is probably the case that bureaucrats are closer to the centres of decision-making in Britain than in the United States, it is certainly true that parties play a much greater role here. American studies often have little to say about local parties, simply because they are often weak or non-existent. On both sides of the Atlantic, however, work has been inclined to centre on the role of political parties at election time, and on the part played by parties in organising members of decision-making elites. The party linkages between citizens and leaders have rarely been examined. For example, besides mobilising voters on election day, what role do local parties play in aggregating and articulating opinion on community matters? How important are party organisations as channels of communication between rank-and-file members and leaders? How do varieties of party system (one-party dominance or two-party competitive) affect public policy? What effects does the presence of strong and cohesive parties have on the policy-making power of bureaucrats? While American research can sometimes ignore these sorts of questions with impunity, the whole question of the importance of local parties must be placed at the centre of British studies of community politics and decision-making.

One startling gap in the American literature is the absence of any systematic empirical work on the role of voluntary organisations in local politics. This is a little curious, to say the least, since voluntary organisations and associations are at the heart of a great deal of theorising about modern society in general, and since pluralist theory in particular is based very largely on the presumed activities of a wide variety of such groups in protecting their interests against the threatened encroachment of other groups and elites. Yet remarkably little empirical work has been published on any aspect of voluntary organisations, including their political activity. Sociologists have been able to produce a large number of well-substantiated generalisations about what kinds of people join organisations, but they have little to say about the organisations themselves. Political scientists have conducted numerous case studies of particular pressure groups and of particular issues involving a small number of pressure groups, but they have usually chosen rather special or spectacular groups and issues, and there is doubt about the extent to which the conclusions are generally applicable to a wide range of groups and issues. Before we can go much further we ought to try to answer a range of general questions about community organisations: how many are there in the average city, what interests do they represent, what proportion are politically active at any given time, what sorts of issues stimulate their political activity, how do they operate as local pressure groups, whom do they contact and with what success, what do they do if they are not successful? These sorts of questions have not been tackled and, indeed, they have never been asked in the first place. However, a small amount of preliminary research in the two countries suggests that it may well be easier to deal with them in Britain than in the United States.

Because of the way in which the community power debate has developed, American literature has concentrated very heavily on the question of the number of elites in any community, the extent to which they compete with one another, and the extent to which their power is specialised or generalised. This focus of attention ignores another question which may be more important for local democracy, namely, the extent to which community elites are responsive and responsible to non-elites. Few doubt that political elites are inevitable to some extent in modern industrial society, but what is important is the way in which elites relate to the mass of ordinary citizens. Can they act pretty much as they wish, or do they have to take into account the needs and demands of citizens if they are to retain their elite positions? This sort of question shifts attention from the number and competitive nature of elites to the relationship between elites and non-elites. Future studies of local politics might well examine the recruitment, behaviour and organisation of elite groups, all of which has been done many times on both sides of the Atlantic, but in the light of the need to understand the ways in which elites interact with citizens. This would take the study of local politics and decision-making into the role of elections, parties and pressure groups in the system of local democracy, and into the ways in which elite policy meets the needs and demands of the wider community.

American community power studies have been caught up very closely with the question of which particular individuals and groups are powerful or powerless. To ask 'Who governs?' is to direct attention on to people and groups, and to direct attention away from the organisational, cultural and historical framework within which decisions are made. Community power studies discuss the importance of mayors, businessmen, industrialists, bankers, newspaper editors, trade union leaders, city bosses, councilmen and city managers. The vocabulary of the studies is made up of words such as 'motives', 'interests', 'behaviour', 'choice' and 'activity'. Rarely does the discussion move to the systems or structural level of explanation, and rarely has attention been given to the way in which social and political structures affect political decisions. Terms like 'organisational imperatives', 'structural conduciveness', 'the funnel of causality' and 'institutional constraints' are rarely used. Political decisions are seen as the end-product of a multitude of individual actions, and there is little sense of the way in which total social situations structure outcomes, and systematically block off some of the alternatives.

This is especially characteristic of the pluralist writing,[25] but it also applies to those who are most critical of the pluralists. Although the original work of Schattsneider discusses the ways in which the mobilisation of bias is inherent within any political structure or organisation, irrespective of which particular set of individuals is in them, the neo-elitist work has tended to consider the ways in which individuals with particular motives and interests may be able to suppress issues. This inevitably directs attention to the possible existence of elites or power elites with non-decision-making capabilities, and overlooks the way in which impersonal political structures place constraints on political life.

Some examples are necessary. Studies of local decision-making usually take the political boundary round the city as a given, and examine what goes on inside this political unit. Yet the drawing of a political boundary is itself a potent political act with all sorts of implications for community decisions, for not infrequently a line is drawn between the city and its suburbs. This is an example of the mobilisation of bias, or rather the institutionalisation of bias, in so far as the division cuts off middle-class suburbs, with money and few problems, from the inner city, which often has little money

---

[25]   Thomas J. Anton, 'Power, Pluralism, and Local Politics', *Administrative Science Quarterly*, Mar 1963, pp. 425-58, and the letters by Dahl and Anton in the following issue.

and a gigantic set of social problems.[26] Political boundaries of this sort are extremely important in the United States because they occur so frequently,[27] but they are also to be found in Britain.

Indeed, the very fragmentation of American local government has great importance for the nature and content of public policy. Dividing up local government into some 80,000 separate units often makes it difficult or virtually impossible to provide collective benefits in the form of planning of public services. There is often no official body large enough or authoritative enough to formulate and apply an overall plan for the metropolitan area, and sometimes there is no agency capable of delivering adequate public services. In the absence of governmental machinery to provide collective benefits and public solutions to urban problems, the population has to rely on private resources and individual solutions — thus the frequently remarked-upon paradox of public squalor amid private affluence. Of course, the people with the private resources to meet these problems are typically middle- and upper-class citizens who, by moving out of the central city and into the suburbs and then creating their own special suburban governments, helped create the problems in the first place. Hence the fragmentation of local government, where it places constraints on the provision of collective benefits and the adoption of public solutions, represents a

---

[26] Some of the economic ramifications are discussed in James Heilbron, 'Poverty and Public Finance in the Older Central Cities', and Jerome Rothenberg, 'Local Decentralisation and the Theory of Optimal Government', both in Matthew Edel and Jerome Rothenberg (eds.), *Readings in Urban Economics* (New York: Macmillan, 1972). For the political background to urban/suburban division, see Robert C. Wood, *Suburbia* (Boston: Houghton Mifflin, 1958). For British work, see Stephen L. Bristow, 'The Criteria for Local Government Reorganisation and Local Autonomy', *Policy and Politics*, Dec 1972, pp. 143-62.

[27] Theodore J. Lowi, in *The End of Liberalism* (New York: W. W. Norton, 1969) pp. 194-9, analyses this problem in his usual masterly way.

form of the mobilisation of bias which generally benefits the middle and upper classes.[28]

On the other hand, it is claimed that fragmentation contributes to local pluralism and hence to local democracy.[29] But this seems to confuse two separate things: the fragmentation of formal decision-making bodies on the one hand, and the proliferation of many informal centres of power on the other. Governmental fragmentation typically seems to lead to powerlessness and immobilism of public bodies, which are either unable to make public decisions at all, or else able only to nibble at crisis problems in a very ineffective way.[30] Fragmented government seems to contribute less to good government than to non-government, but then, as I have already argued, the slogan 'Good government is no government' has a special appeal to those who can solve their own problems with their own resources. At any rate, this form of government should not be confused with organisational pluralism in the shape of a plurality of private organisations such as churches, trade unions, political parties, professional

[28] For evidence supporting the argument in this paragraph, see Charles R. Adrian, 'Narrow Class Concerns and Urban Unrest', *American Politics Quarterly*, July 1973, pp. 397-404; G. Ross Stephens, 'The Power Grid of the Metropolis', in Frederick M. Wirt (ed.), *Future Directions in Community Power Research* (Berkeley: Institute of Governmental Studies, 1971) p. 135; Oliver P. Williams, *Metropolitan Political Analysis* (New York: Free Press, 1971) p. 51, and 'Life Style Values and Political Decentralisation in Metropolitan Areas', *Southwest Social Science Quarterly*, Dec 1967, pp. 299-310; Terry N. Clark, 'Centralisation Encourages Public Goods, but Decentralisation Generates Separable Goods', Research Paper No. 39 of the Comparative Study of Community Decision-Making.

[29] Robert Dahl is the most notable exponent of this theory and his most recent statement is in *Democracy in the United States: Promise and Performance* (Chicago: Rand McNally, 1972) chap. 17.

[30] This aspect of American local government is discussed very thoroughly in a two-part article by L. J. Sharpe, 'American Democracy Reconsidered', *British Journal of Political Science*, Jan 1973, pp. 1-28 and Apr 1973, pp. 130-67. See also Robert L. Bish and Robert Warren, 'Scale and Monopoly Problems in Urban Government Services', *Urban Affairs Quarterly*, Sep 1972, pp. 97-122.

associations, business organisations, and community clubs and organisations of all kinds. It is difficult to imagine a democratic political system which did not contain a highly differentiated system of organisations of these kinds, for they are one of the main social mechanisms which help ensure the responsiveness and responsibility of the elites. Yet organisational pluralism is clearly not a sufficient condition of democracy. The relationship between pluralist democracy and organisational pluralism is mediated by the type of government with which the organisations are involved.

The typically fragmented city government of the United States is most generally complemented by a high degree of organisational pluralism. In Lowi's neat, incisive phrase: 'There are many publics, but no polity'.[31] The result is a situation in which the private resources of private organisations and individuals are given maximum room to pursue their private solutions to their own private problems. The resources which are most in evidence are the middle- and upper-class groupings which are best able to organise themselves to protect their own interests. As a result, fragmented government structure combined with organisational pluralism is a formula which encourages private middle-class solutions to middle-class problems, and non-decisions for other kinds of problems.

In Britain, and in many other European countries, local government is more unified and has greater power. It is capable, in principle if not always in actual fact, of delivering collective benefits and implementing public solutions to public problems. As a result, the many private organisations which exist are inclined to exert pressure on public authorities in order to influence public policy so far as it affects their own private interests. This system of pressure group politics most probably benefits the better organised, that is, the middle- and upper-class sections of society, more than it benefits the less well organised and the totally unorganised. Yet when local government can distribute collective benefits because it is endowed with powers to do so, and when these powers encompass a broad geographical area and range of

[31] Lowi, *The End of Liberalism*, p. 197.

governmental functions, then groups with relatively few resources will be encouraged to use them in order to prise collective benefits out of the system, thereby attaining their goals and adding to their own resources in the process. This is the way in which the Labour Party, the trade unions and the various working-class organisations operate in almost every British city.

Yet this system contains its own special form of the mobilisation of bias. The whole structure of British politics, and no less of British local politics, has crystallised around working-class and middle-class interests. People or groups who do not fit into this system are, to all intents and purposes, politically exiled. Until very recently, they have been a small minority of ideological deviants on the left and the right, and even these people have been classified according to the dominant organising principle of British politics — the left and the right. Now, however, we have an important section of society who either will not or cannot be accommodated by the working-class/socialist and the middle-class/conservative camps. Coloured people will not find it possible to break their way into the political system unless it undergoes some fairly major structural alterations, and those alterations are going to be accomplished at the cost of political anguish and possibly violence. Meanwhile the class-based political system continues to be a non-decision-making structure so far as questions of coloured welfare are concerned. Apart from the obvious importance for future politics, a study of race and non-decision-making might make a useful comparison with the American work.[32]

One of the most important lessons to come out of the American experience has been left until last. The early community power studies treated their cities as if they were city-states with autonomous and and independent policy-making powers. Rarely were the links between local, state and federal government examined.[33] British research has generally started

[32]   See Ira Katznelson, *Black Men, White Cities* (London: Oxford Univ. Press, 1973); and Michael Hill and Ruth Issacharoff, *Community Action and Race Relations* (London: Oxford Univ. Press, 1971).

[33]   Mark Kesselman, 'Research Perspectives in Comparative Local Politics: Pitfalls and Prospects', *Comparative Urban Research*, Spring 1972, pp. 10-30.

from the opposite assumption with the idea that there is little call to study local politics simply because central government pays the local piper and calls just about every note of his tune. Since decisions are made in Whitehall and Westminster, there is no sense in looking at local politics and decision-making. Recent work has questioned this set of assumptions, and although the evidence is still far from conclusive, it does suggest that local authorities may have more latitude for independent policy-making than has generally been assumed.[34] Of course, to raise questions about local government autonomy immediately puts the whole research question in a comparative context, because any attempt to discover the extent of local variation means comparing local authorities.[35]

The recent trend in British research, however, is away from comparative studies and in favour of depth studies of particular cities. This work has already turned up a great deal of fascinating and enlightening material and our understanding of British politics would be much the poorer without it. But in many ways these case studies have put the local politics horse before the comparative local government cart. There is only limited use in studying a particular city in depth unless we know something about how it fits into the overall national pattern, and at the moment we know rather little about the overall national pattern. Since the present writer's current research is open to this line of criticism, it seems only fair to take it as an example. A study of Birmingham shows the presence of a very large number of voluntary organisations, many of which are politically active in trying to influence public policy. An examination of the groups tells us a great deal about the political world of community organisations, but without a comparative study we cannot tell (*a*) how Birmingham compares with other cities in terms of the number and strength of local pressure groups, or (*b*) whether these groups seem to have any effect on public policy, or (*c*)

[34] Cf. Noel Boaden, *Urban Policy Making* (Cambridge: Cambridge Univ. Press, 1971); and John Dearlove, *The Politics of Policy in Local Government* (Cambridge: Cambridge Univ. Press, 1973).
[35] Local variations do not prove the existence of local autonomy because they may be the intended consequence of central government policy.

in what areas they are effective or ineffective, or (*d*) what
sorts of factors might explain these local findings. If local
policy is set by national government, then much of the
ground is cut away from beneath a study of local pressure
groups. But if Birmingham policies are special in some respects, and if local pressure groups are special in the same respects, then we might tentatively conclude that the groups
have something to do with the policy.

Here lies what is probably the best strategic use of comparative studies of local government policy. Until we have
some idea of how cities fit into the general pattern, case
studies of particular cities are very limited in the kinds of
generalisations they can provide. On the other hand, comparative studies on a broad enough scale to yield dependable
conclusions about the overall pattern will not be able to tell
us much about the political processes which underlie public
policy. Having done the comparative studies, we can *then*
start selecting particular cases on strong theoretical and
empirical grounds. There is nothing wrong with case studies,
so long as we know what they are cases of. Careful and
sensitive case studies of the internal political processes of
cities must be complemented by equally careful and sensitive
comparative studies of a whole range of different types of
cities.

On the Study of Urban Electoral Behaviour

Jeffrey Stanyer

There has been a tendency in recent years to devalue the role of local elections in British local government, partly in reaction to the excessive claims of traditional supporters of local democracy. The nineteenth-century view of the latter is untenable in the light of the evidence of uncontested seats, one-party dominant systems, consistently low turnouts in some areas, and the highly selective nature of local council membership, and it contained an obviously erroneous view of the position of the elected member. Attention has therefore tended to focus on such factors as the roles of chief officers and the agencies of central government, the urban poor — especially underprivileged minorities — and aggressive capitalism in the form of the property interests of urban society.

This devaluation is, however, unjustified. It arises partly from unrealistic expectations about the *direct* influence of local electoral behaviour on local decision-making. But it can be reversed only by adopting a better approach to the study and interpretation of local electoral behaviour.[1] Though local elections can rarely be shown to have a direct and immediate effect on any individual decision of a local authority, a proper analysis will show how they fix some of the major parameters of the local political systems — in effect, factors which enter indirectly in many, if not all, aspects of local authority behaviour. Thus, local elections can be restored to their rightful place in the accepted picture of urban political processes only if the relationships between local electoral

[1] Most of the general considerations which apply to the study of urban electoral behaviour also apply to the study of all local electoral behaviour. Not only can the latter be described in terms of a number of dimensions or aspects which are relevant to the most rural and the most urban areas, but *urbanisation* is itself a phenomenon which shows infinite gradations.

behaviour and these factors, parameters or constraints on decision-making are identified. The discovery of the ways in which these relationships may be studied is, however, at the end of a long series of methodological considerations.

There are two reasons why local elections are not given their proper part in the understanding of urban politics. Firstly, traditional students of local government — in fact the great majority — have tended both to be unfamiliar with modern approaches in the social sciences and to refuse to remedy this defect. There is a useful study of the history of local elections[2] and many good accounts of local electoral law,[3] but generally the traditionalists have been unwilling to exploit the potentialities of local elections as data for modern methods.

Secondly, political scientists well qualified to undertake the right sort of research have generally been either unaware or contemptuous of local government. But it can be shown that local elections have great potential in at least three distinct areas of modern political science as well as in more traditional and narrowly defined local government studies.

There are two vital considerations in modern behavioural studies. The data studied must contain both sufficient numbers of cases and sufficient variation within the set for the purposes of the investigator. Local elections score very highly on both counts. The number of elections is very large because of the number of authorities (and electoral areas into which they are divided) and the frequency of elections. Data relating to local elections also contain a great deal of 'natural' variation, which is created by a host of factors, including differences in electoral law, varying relations between law and social factors, and different political situations.

Prima facie, therefore, local elections are extremely important to the student of electoral behaviour in general. They are also a promising field for comparative analysis, for only at the local level are there sufficient cases for modern methods

[2]   B. Keith-Lucas, *The English Local Government Franchise* (Oxford: Basil Blackwell, 1952).

[3]   A. N. Schofield, *Local Government Elections*, 4th Ed. (London: Shaw & Sons, 1962).

and forms of research.[4] Traditional political sociology, which was simply the study of the influence of social factors on political behaviour, also required large numbers of cases. In each of the three areas above, local elections also have the significant advantage that the comparability of data is much greater as differences in law and culture are much less.

The local government specialist also needs to study local elections properly because their existence is one of the distinguishing features of local government compared with other forms of local administration of public services. To a large extent the 'theory' of local government is based on the role of local elections, both in its nineteenth-century form and in its application in developing countries.[5]

Despite the sheer quantity and availability of local electoral data, the number of studies that are avowedly behavioural is quite small and many are not rigorously empirical even in intention. A critical review of work on local electoral behaviour undertaken in the mid-1960s revealed that the field had been largely neglected[6] and that few studies of more than elementary sophistication had been published. Since that time more has been published, but the overwhelming impression is still one of relative neglect.

The trouble has been partly that studies of local elections tend to fall into one of four clearly defined categories, each of which has its own particular 'demons' — serious technical problems that are often not confronted by the writer.[7]

Some pieces of research might best be described as 'current history' — accounts in chronological order of the course

---

4   J. Stanyer, 'Comparative Government', chap. 5 in H. V. Wiseman (ed.), *Political Science* (London: Routledge & Kegan Paul, 1967); J. Blondel, *An Introduction to Comparative Government* (London: Weidenfeld & Nicolson, 1969).

5   B. C. Smith, 'The Justification of Local Government', chap. 27 in L. D. Feldman and M. D. Goldrick (eds.), *Politics and Government of Urban Canada* (Agincourt, Ontario: Methuen, 1969); L. J. Sharpe, 'Theories and Values of Local Government', *Political Studies*, June 1970, pp. 153-74.

6   J. Stanyer, 'Local Electoral Behaviour', paper presented to the Annual Conference of the Political Studies Association, Univ. of Sussex, Apr 1968.

7   The following discussion is a summary of the account in Stanyer, ibid.

of an election, with varying amounts of generalisation and explanation. The oldest type of rigorous research is the analysis of aggregrate data on local elections provided for all local authorities other than parishes by Table V of the Registrar-General's *Statistical Review of England and Wales, Part II*, published annually, which contains standardised data on two aspects of electoral behaviour — *turnout* and *seats contested*. Information on these two aspects and many more has been gathered for the electoral areas of individual authorities, and subjected to the same and more elaborate analysis. Finally there have been some, though surprisingly few, studies of individual electors and candidates using interview and questionnaire methods.

The difficulties in each of these drive the student of local elections progressively from one to another. Studies of the course of an individual election tend to be diffuse and inconclusive, often having a marked journalistic flavour. Though the background knowledge they provide may be useful in other types of study, many researchers have regarded them as only part of wider projects. The need for comparison as a basis for understanding thus presses the student towards the collection of standardised data for a number of authorities.

Prior to the Second World War this was difficult because of the problems of collecting information for areas other than those near to the researcher's own location.[8] The publication of the Registrar-General's statistics annually since 1945-6 has made this type of study much easier, but the earlier insights have not been pursued. Among the difficulties it encounters the most important is the fact that the same gross figures relating to turnout and seats contested have very different significances in different electoral systems — a point which cannot be examined by this method.

Students have thus been pressed towards greater disaggregation through the use of data relating to the individual electoral areas within authorities. This method has two advan-

8   E. C. Rhodes, 'The Exercise of the Franchise in London', *Political Quarterly*, Jan — Mar 1938, pp. 113-19, and 'Voting at Municipal Elections', *Political Quarterly*, Apr — June 1938, pp. 271-80.

tages: it generates information relating to a much wider range of aspects of local electoral behaviour, and the meaning of the variables studied and the interpretation of the results are much less questionable.

The demand for yet further disaggregation arises because the above method generates a large amount of data about candidates and council members but virtually none about electors and activists. The use of questionnaire and interview methods enables one to collect additional data of a different sort about candidates and members and data about those who do not appear in the published material — activists other than candidates, and electors and voters.

In practice such studies have been much less satisfactory than was hoped in advance. They have been particularly prone to the difficulties that affect all interview methods: for instance, only a few have administered properly the question 'Did you vote in the local election held on . . . ?' Panel studies in this field are almost centainly impossible; because of lesser publicity in local elections, interviews beforehand will alert the panel to the existence of the elections which they might otherwise not have noticed.[9]

Even if the technical problems are overcome, it is hard to see how such methods can make more than a marginal contribution to the central issues of the study of urban politics. This is because each study is so constrained by limitations of time and space that it is not possible to answer the questions asked. For instance, a survey of individuals cannot do more

[9]   A survey of published interview studies suggests that the timing of the research is of vital importance. The Clapham study obtained a percentage reporting having voted very close to actual turnout, whilst the Newcastle-under-Lyme and Sheffield studies were wildly wrong. The former took place less than two weeks after the election whilst the latter two had allowed nine and six months respectively to elapse: L. J. Sharpe, *A Metropolis Votes*, Greater London Paper No. 8 (London: L.S.E., 1962); F. Bealey *et al. Constituency Politics* (London: Faber, 1965); W. Hampton, *Democracy and Community* (London: Oxford Univ. Press, 1970). The first Newcastle study, which was into voting intentions, found that 13 per cent of the sample changed their minds about voting between one question and another: F. Bealey and D. J. Bartholomew, 'The Local Elections in Newcastle-under-Lyme, May 1958', *British Journal of Sociology* , Sep, Dec 1962, pp. 273-85, 350-68.

than provide a snapshot of the situation at that point in time
at that place. This will be consistent with a great variety of
patterns of social and political change and with different
states of affairs in other areas. As social and political change
are likely to be a major preoccupation in urban political
studies, it is easy to see that this method is of only marginal
value in answering some of the central questions.

There is, however, a much more important problem which
occurs in all four types of research and which in the long run
none of them can solve. The technical problems of each type
can either be answered by more accurate and careful work, or
circumvented by a reduction of the claims made for the
findings, but this basic logical difficulty — which is shared
with all research aiming at explanation in the social sciences
— is always fatal unless directly defeated.

Only a small amount of sensitivity in the layman is required for an awareness to develop that all sorts of influences
may and do bear on social behaviour; such an awareness will
be strengthened by an examination of writings on local elections which reveals a whole range of factors which have been
either used in research or the subject of speculation as determinants of local electoral behaviour.[10] These potential factors or influences may be grouped into four main categories:

A-factors: social, economic, geographical, etc., characteristics
   of the area, often with a historical dimension, which in
   effect constitute the background environment of the
   council;
B-factors: constitutional, political and legal factors which are
   either part of the environment or the rules which govern
   behaviour;
C-factors: the psychological characteristics of individuals —
   traits, attitudes, motives, abilities, etc.;
D-factors: those which derive from the fact that human
   beings appear to be rational calculators.

Once several factors are thought to be relevant to the

[10]   Many of these factors can also be found in American research,
   which in general has been vastly more rigorous and elaborate. See,
   for instance, E. C. Banfield and J. Q. Wilson, *City Politics*
   (Cambridge, Mass.: Harvard Univ. Press and M.I.T. Press, 1963) and
   the books and articles referred to in their footnotes.

understanding of a situation, the problem arises both of a framework in which to assess their relative affects and of a weighting system through which assignment of importance can be made. Any analysis which deals with factors drawn from all four categories — as studies of urban politics do — must deal with the problems which arise when different variables have different characteristics.

A-factors usually generate continuous variables, sometimes with a definite range and sometimes infinite in one or both directions. C-factors also tend to be thought of as continuous and infinite variables, though the level of measurement of their units is often controversial. Legal and constitutional factors, however, are often dichotomous or trichotomous variables of only a nominal level of measurement. Political factors are sometimes discrete and sometimes continuous variables. And the concepts of rationality generate a completely different set of variables.

Other characteristics of variables are equally the source of difficulties. For instance, a constant cannot explain a variable, and if what is to be understood is a stochastic process, then the factors accounting for it must contain at least one probabilistic assumption. Many factors create variables at the level of the individual and the level of the group or collectivity. Thus, explanations have to bridge the gap between the individual and aggregate levels of analysis — to avoid the ecological fallacy. Some variables change their nature over time and space: for instance, they may be constants in any given election but variables in a set of elections.[11]

One consequence of the above considerations is especially pertinent in the study of local electoral behaviour. For purposes of research the web of social life is divided up into manageable sections. This is both a necessary and a dangerous procedure. The danger arises when it becomes desirable to put together some of the separate parts and the attempt fails, leaving knowledge of social behaviour in watertight compartments.

[11] Most of these points about levels of measurement and the relations between individual and aggregate data are standard points which are discussed in most statistics textbooks. See, for instance, H.M. Blalock, *Social Statistics* (New York: McGraw-Hill, 1960).

Local electoral processes are essentially *end-on* to other social processes. They are rooted in the processes of everyday life and are part of the inputs into the internal processes of the council itself. They may also be parallel to other processes, such as those of partisan organisation.

The implication of this is that the analysis of one process should not be inconsistent with the analyses of the others; the conclusions of one become the premises of the other. As, in general, factors carry their basic characteristics forward to the 'next' subject, it is vital that there be ways of reconciling the differences likely to arise when two processes are married. At a practical level it is important that no description and explanation be bound to the materiality of any particular set of activities without being capable of an interpretation in all adjacent ones.

When studies of local elections were in their earliest stages there were a number of choices open to the researcher which have now in effect been closed. Though electoral behaviour may be treated as an independent or a dependent variable, it was generally treated as the latter. Research was aimed at discovering what sort of factors produced different types of behaviour, and attention was concentrated on either background factors of type A or simple political variables of type B. Analyses moved too easily from the aggregate to the individual level, as when apathy — a characteristic of the individual — was inferred from low turnouts — a group characteristic.

Four major aspects of electoral behaviour have usually been selected as the dependent variables to be studied: *partisanship, competitiveness, turnout* and *selectivity*. But these have not been equally popular and it may be thought that there has been an undue emphasis on *turnout*. As the latter is technically the best of the dependent variables, this was sensible when there was little or no effort made to relate elections to such factors as council decision-making, officer/members relations, provision of services, etc. — in other words, to treat electoral behaviour as an independent variable.

The explanatory variables chosen in the traditional studies involved a more limited notion of political sociology than would be accepted now. For instance, the most popular factors were those of population — size, density, mobility and composition. Political factors considered were also fairly simple ones — measures of partisan conflict such as *marginality*.[12]

The result is that the subjects that are of vital concern to the student of urban politics — the relationships between the urban socio-geographical environment and the behaviour of local political institutions — are left to the field of speculation. In the traditional local government literature there can be found many beliefs about the influence of aspects of elections on the behaviour of local authorities, but virtually no hard evidence.

The alternative way to approach urban elections is to construct a *theoretical model* whose task it is to explain a wide range of local political behaviour in the centre of which are local elections. Words such as 'model', 'theory' and 'system' are used with a variety of meanings in the social sciences — often interchangeably; but only if they are given the highly specific and precisely stated meaning prescribed below will they have the functions required of them in this context.[13]

A model is a deductive system containing only abstract symbols and those logical constants and logical operators necessitated by the rules of inference belonging to the particular system. Using a model is therefore an exercise in applied logic, but commonly it will be thought of as applied mathematics. A theory is an interpretation of a model in which some of the symbols in the model are given an empirical meaning. Thus, some of the variables are said to correspond to factors in the data which are to be understood in the light of the theory. In reverse, the model is said to be a

[12] A. H. Birch, 'The Habit of Voting', *Manchester School of Economics and Social Science*, Jan 1950 pp. 75-82; Political and Economic Planning, 'Voting for Local Councils', *Planning*, May 1955 pp. 49-64; K. Newton, 'Turnout and Marginality in Local Elections', *British Journal of Political Science*, Apr 1972, pp. 251-5.

[13] J. Stanyer, 'Electoral Behaviour in Local Government: A Model of a Two-Party System', *Political Studies*, June 1970, pp. 187-204, and 'Social and Rational Models of Man', *Advancement of Science*, June 1970, pp. 399-405.

symbolic or canonical representation of the theory. A system is a special type of model, in which one or more variables show homeostatic features, that is, a tendency to keep a constant value, or to vary only within a small range, despite wide variations in other factors.

To explain why it is that only this type of activity will meet the needs described above is beyond the scope of this paper and would certainly require a whole chapter by itself. In what follows it is intended to *illustrate* the approach, not to explain or justify it directly.

A MODEL OF URBAN ELECTIONS

The choice of the bases for the construction of such a theoretical model is strongly influenced by two factors: it is in practical terms easier to start with a *rational* model of man[14] than to add rational elements to a social model, and the model must at some point make contact with the most salient features of the urban political environment. The foundation of a useful model lies in the role of *partisanship*.

British urban elections are dominated by partisanship, that is, the overt attachment of electors and activists alike to a political party, usually one of the two major national parties, but sometimes the Liberals or a minor national party, or a purely local party. Partisan attachments form a key factor in the understanding and analysis of all aspects of urban local politics, and nowhere more obviously than in elections. It clearly affects the other three elements of electoral behaviour – competitiveness, turnout and the composition of local councils – and helps to determine the character of the political institutions in which decision-making takes place.

Partisanship is also something that can easily be interpreted in the categories of rational action: the choice of

14   *Rationality* in this context is used in a special sense. When behaviour is thought of as reasonable, justified, correct (or any similar adjective) this will be because it is based on a defensible view of the way the world works and because it promotes the values of the actor. Any of these words could be used to refer to the conception of man as doing things for reasons; *rational* is chosen because of its connotation of rigorous calculation, a process which relates the facts and values of the individual to the choice of behaviour.

parties, changes in allegiance, disillusionment, etc., can be pictured either as a consequence of the values or of the perceptions of individual citizens, or some combination of these. Such an interpretation is reinforced by the way individuals themselves talk about their party allegiance, or lack of it.

There are many ways of showing the importance of political parties in British urban local government. The simplest way is to examine the table on the political composition of councils, published in the *Municipal Year Book* annually since 1956, except for 1960. For instance, in 1962 it reveals that the central cities of the large urbanised areas (Birmingham, Liverpool, Manchester, Leeds, etc.) and the free-standing cities (Nottingham, Leicester, Plymouth, Norwich, etc.) were all virtually monopolised by Labour and Conservative council members. An even stronger impression of the significance of the major parties is given by the analysis published each year before and after the local elections by *The Economist*. This is oriented almost entirely to changes in national party fortunes and to changes in party control of councils. A summary of the position in each of the types of local authority in respect of party control has been included in most of the R.I.P.A.'s annual surveys of developments in public administration.[15]

In most of the towns of over 50,000 population, partisanship meant support for either Labour or Conservative, but occasionally it meant the Liberals or a purely local party. For instance, in 1961 Liberals were over 20 per cent of the council in the county boroughs of Blackpool, Halifax, Huddersfield, Rochdale and Southport, and in some places the non-Labour members were known by special local titles: Citizens' Party (Bristol, Barnsley), Municipal Association (Dewsbury, Kingston-upon-Hull), Progressives (Doncaster) and Rent and Ratepayers (Gateshead).

The pervasiveness of party in urban politics can be shown in less obvious ways. The table on p. 243 of Butler and Freeman gives the number of seats won in borough elections

---

[15]   B. C. Smith and J. Stanyer, 'Administrative Developments in 1970: A Survey', *Public Administration*, Winter 1971, p.431.

since 1949 by the various parties,[16] and if the Labour percentage of the combined Labour and Conservative percentages is correlated with the party's standing in the national Gallup Polls for *any* of the months January to April, then remarkably similar and strong predictors of the former are discovered. Party also influences the social composition of councils: were it not for Labour candidatures, the small working-class element in urban local authorities would virtually disappear.[17]

Even though in national politics urban and rural constituencies do not show any evidence of significant differences in behaviour, it is clear that at the local level they are in marked contrast. It would be wrong to draw a hard-and-fast line between rural and urban areas, but if the two poles of the rural — urban continuum (based on such factors as economic activity and size and density of population) are compared, it will be seen that partisanship is the characteristic that most clearly distinguishes them.

For instance, party intervention in local elections will have dramatic effects on the pattern of contested elections, that is, electoral competition. In rural areas elections are often largely uncontested and the exceptions are obviously created by processes with large stochastic elements in them. A full-blooded party system, however, involves a commitment by each party to contest each seat, irrespective of the chances of it being won. Though there is also a tendency for the minority party to 'wither' in the one-party dominant areas, and thus not to contest all seats, the general consequences of partisanship can be seen by comparing the figures for seats contested given annually by the Registrar-General for county boroughs and rural districts, or for urbanised and non-urbanised administrative counties.

In most of the large urban areas of Britain local electoral

16   D. Butler and J. Freeman, *British Political facts, 1900-1967*, 2nd ed. (London: Macmillan, 1968).
17   Much of the evidence for these and for subsequent descriptions of urban politics is contained in unpublished research by the present author. For reasons of space it is not possible to recount this and other evidence, but the claims made are not in any sense controversial.

behaviour exhibits a common structure. It is easiest to detect this in the biggest cities where the two major parties dominate the political scene and where the partisan attachments of electors and council members are strongest. This common structure will be presented as a theoretical model whose elements are in practice found in varying degrees in particular localities, and therefore whose explanatory value also varies from place to place.

Firstly, it is assumed that the two major national parties (the 'reds' and 'blacks', in a non-country-specific terminology) monopolise the locality's party system; that is, only they put up candidates and command support among the electorate. In the most austere version it is also assumed that there are only two parties at the national level.

Secondly, it is assumed that the fortunes of the two parties in each locality (relative to each other) are largely determined by the fortunes of their national counterparts. The form of the relationship, however, need not be the same in different areas: on the contrary, it is likely to differ systematically in significant ways.

Thirdly, it is assumed that the local election system is the familiar British first-past-the-post system, with a considerable number of single-member constituencies (usually called 'wards'). There is no definite minimum number of wards, but the fewer there are the more likely that other factors will structure the pattern of elections.

One of the consequences of having a British type of electoral system in a two-party situation is that any change in popular support is magnified in changes in seats won in an election. This phenomenon was once analysed in terms of a 'cube law', and although that has now largely fallen into disuse, the facts that it purported to describe still remain.[18] Thus, in some situations for every 1 per cent a party gains in votes relative to the other it is likely to gain 2 per cent of seats. In other places this gain may be of the order of 3 per cent or more. Thus, for example, if a party increased its share

[18] E. R. Tufte, 'The Relationship between Seats and Votes in Two-Party Systems', *American Political Science Review*, June 1973, pp. 540-54.

of the vote by 10 per cent, and the seats/votes relation was 3, then it would gain an extra 30 seats in a 100-seat council.

The relationship between national and local support for a political party, though a constant in each locality, is a variable in a cross-section of authorities. It may be as low as 0·5 in some areas and as high as 1·5 in others; that is, as a party's national support changes, in some areas its local support will change at only half that rate and in others at one and a half times. For example, if a party increased in national support by 10 per cent, it would in the first case increase by only 5 and in the second by 15 per cent its local support.

These two relationships may be combined to create a *national/local multiplier* which relates changes in seats won in an election to changes in the national standing of the party. This is the product of the two above relationships; thus it is conceivable that the value of this multiplier will be as low as 1·5 or as high as 4·5. It is likely, however, that in many areas it will lie somewhere between these two extremes, perhaps between 2·0 and 3·0. This means that as the Gallup Polls show a party increasing its support nationally by 10 per cent, its local counterparts will be winning between 20 and 30 extra seats in a 100-seat council.

The above is a verbal presentation of something that is in essence a logical system and thus capable of symbolic representation. Indeed, this is a necessary next step, as its properties can be exploited only if it is cast in full deductive form. It is much easier to do this than many timid political scientists believe.

Firstly, to say that two parties monopolise a party system is simply to say that between them they hold all the seats, have all the candidates and are supported by all electors. If the two parties are denoted by subscripts 1 and 2 respectively, and N and L stand for national and local support, then the equations below express this monopoly exactly:

$$N_1 + N_2 = 100$$
$$L_1 + L_2 = 100$$

Similarly, if S stands for seats won in an election, then

$$S_1 + S_2 = 100$$

Secondly, the description of the relationship between national and local support for a political party implies unequivocally that it is a linear one; that is, the formula which describes it generates a set of points on the graph which can be joined up as a straight line. The same is true of the account of the relationship between seats won and votes within each locality. Thus the formula for the simple linear relationship may be used to specify the two relationships:

$$L_1 = aN_1 + b$$
$$S_1 = cL_1 + d.$$

These five axioms are all that are required to construct the deductive system necessary to analyse the central features of urban electoral behaviour.[19] The model generates the measures that are needed to provide the links to analyses of other processes of urban politics and creates a framework into which the various types of relevant factor mentioned above can be fitted. This is done simply by using the processes of deductive reasoning that are implicit in the simple mathematics of the axioms.

Firstly, by substitution using the first three axioms the formulae for the relationships involving the second party can be derived from the last two axioms. Thus:

$$L_2 = 100 - L_1$$
$$= 100 - (aN_1 + b)$$
$$= 100 - a(100 - N_2) - b$$

Secondly, by the combination of the fourth and fifth axioms,

$$S_1 = c(aN_1 + b) + d$$
$$= caN_1 + cb + d$$

Ca is in fact the *national/local multiplier.*

---

[19] In a more abstract theoretical analysis the fourth and fifth axioms would be derived from more basic assumptions about individual behaviour, but for the purposes of this chapter this is not necessary as the analysis can proceed properly as it stands. See J. Stanyer, 'Local Support for National Political Parties', *Political Studies*, Sep 1970, pp. 395-9, for an account of the model's theoretical foundations.

The model also generates a measure of two different sorts of *bias* within the system. By substituting 50 for N_1 and subtracting the resultant L_1 from 50, one arrives at the value of a factor which measures the extent to which the locality departs from the national pattern. Thus the national/local bias is calculated thus:

$$\text{bias } N/L = 50 - (a50 + b)$$

The same operation defines the bias in the local electoral system, thus:

$$\text{bias } L/S = 50 - (c50 + d),$$

THE BASES OF PARTISANSHIP

The observed distribution of partisan local political systems can easily be related to a rational model of man; thus the analysis above is based on such a model.

It is fairly easy to establish that local politics becomes 'nationalised' as the size of population of the area increases: the larger the local authority, the greater the probability that its political system will be dominated by the two national parties. This needs to be qualified by the factor of location. The size of the local authority is operative in conjunction with its situation in relation to other authorities. Thus a small urban district located a long way from any centre of population will be non-partisan, whilst an authority of the same size wedged between two county boroughs may well be completely dominated by the major parties.

The most striking fact about partisan voting — that is, voting for a candidate *because* he is the nominee of a particular party — is that it simplifies decision-making and thus reduces its costs. The alternatives are either to vote in the light of some other simple factor, such as religion, race or language — all of which could fulfil the same electoral function as partisan identification — or to vote in the light of a knowledge of the personal characteristics of individual candidates, such as honesty, sobriety and intelligence. As the other simple factors are not generally important in British politics, party attachment is the only alternative to personal voting.

The feasibility of the latter is a function of the degree to which knowledge of individuals in the locality is acquired as a result of the social processes of daily life. This itself is a function of the degree to which the interactions these processes generate are closed and continuous. If interaction between individuals in the locality is frequent and pervasive, and interaction between these and outsiders sporadic, then the social processes of daily life will bring into existence a considerable body of general social knowledge about individuals.

Large urban areas tend to be areas of great personal mobility; commuting is only one aspect of this, though an important one. Shopping and recreation external to the area in which one lives grow in significance the larger the city. Residential change itself tends to increase as it is possible to change one's home without changing one's job. This sort of change is particularly important as it destroys the social knowledge acquired in the past. Any geographical mobility will serve to reduce the extent to which individuals in a locality interact with each other rather than with outsiders, and thus to reduce the social knowledge which would sustain non-partisan voting.

An increase in the size of the locality has a similar effect: it reduces the probability that any individual will have a personal knowledge of any other as a result of the processes of everyday life. The larger the community, the more the system of interactions becomes disjointed or disconnected.[20]

A similar analysis can be made from the point of view of the potential candidate. In the small stable community the resources needed to create and run an electoral organisation may well be found within the family itself, or at least within the immediate circle of friends. Indeed, an electoral organisation may be redundant in that 'electioneering' is taking place

---

[20] These same aspects of city life are the ones chosen by many urban sociologists as the significant factors, particularly those who stress the disenchantment and alienation that they believe the city produces in its inhabitants. See, for instance, Banfield and Wilson, *City Politics*, esp. chap. 4 and pp. 48 ff. Similar nineteenth-century attitudes can be found in B. I. Coleman (ed.), *The Idea of the City in Nineteenth Century Britain* (London: Routledge & Kegan Paul, 1973).

continuously because every interaction may have an effect on other people's perception and evaluation of the individual.

Such a form of electioneering and electoral organisation becomes increasingly difficult as the size of area and personal geographical mobility grow. Elections become expensive in money terms, as well as in terms of voluntary labour. Partisan identification thus reduces the costs of standing for election, both in financial and organisational respects.

The above account of the mechanisms underlying the distribution of partisanship in local government relates the analysis of electoral behaviour to a set of *A-factors* — the sort of factors that are used in general discussions of urban life, including the pessimistic 'doomsday' fears for the future of urban society. There is also some evidence that partisanship is a cost-reducing strategy for voters.

Firstly, where partisan elections coincide with multi-member seats the result is a marked reduction in the proportion of unused votes. In non-partisan elections when each elector has several votes, all of which need not be used, it is quite common for a high proportion of these not to be cast. Although multi-seat wards and partisan elections exist uneasily together, their conjunction is a temporary phenomenon in partial renewal systems when a 'clean sweep' election takes place following a redistribution, and this produces a pattern of unused votes quite different from that familiar to the student of non-partisanship.

Secondly, in these same multi-member wards, if the votes for running mates of the same party are compared it will often be found that there is very little dispersion of support. Again, the student of non-partisanship will find this unfamiliar as the typical independent election scatters votes across a wide range, rather than bunching groups of candidates. There is an asymmetry here in that though a wide dispersion of votes for running mates is not consistent with party voting, close support for candidates of the same party could conceal a great deal of electoral 'indiscipline'.

Not only is there evidence that the model is based on the social processes of large-scale urban society, but the conditions for its applicability are met in many British cities. Firstly, a large proportion of the contests are straight fights

between Labour and Conservative; there are virtually no uncontested wards and only a handful of independents and
other party nominees for most of the time. When others
stand they tend to get only a small percentage of the votes.
The consequence is that in most areas the two major parties
have tended to monopolise council seats. Secondly, if the
votes for one party are correlated with its standing in one of
the national opinion polls at the time of the local elections, it
is found that the latter is a reasonably good explanatory
factor for variations in the former. Thirdly, if seats won in a
succession of elections are correlated with votes for one party
in those elections, a strong relationship, often approximating
to the 'cube law', is discovered.

So far attention has been concentrated on the logic of the
model of electoral behaviour which lies at the heart of many
urban political systems, with a brief account of the 'model of
man' that is assumed to be the foundation of the analysis.
But as was stressed earlier, electoral processes are 'end-on' to
many other social and political processes; no analysis can be
regarded as to any degree useful unless it provides for the
interrelation of these. Instead, however, of discussing these in
the abstract, they will be examined in the context of the new
local government system which came into existence in
England and Wales fully on 1 April 1974. This system departs
from the traditional one, in relation to which the model was
developed, in a number of significant ways, and as theoretical
models are predictive by nature it is interesting to apply it to
a situation which is developing rapidly.

It should be remarked at this point that the following
discussion presupposes the existence of a number of other
models, of other aspects of local political behaviour, which
for reasons of space have been omitted here.

URBAN POLITICS IN THE NEW LOCAL GOVERNMENT SYSTEM

The new local government system differs from the old in a
number of ways that are highly relevant to the study of local
politics in urban areas. In what follows no attempt is made to
give a complete account of local government reform, but

only to draw attention to the salient features of the changes which relate to the model of electoral behaviour.

Firstly, the county borough has disappeared as a type of local authority. Most of the medium and large towns, whether they were set in a mainly rural or small town hinterland or were traditional subdivisions of a conurbation, had their own all-inclusive or all-purpose local authority; they were not parts of any multi-tier system. The self-sufficiency of their urban political systems has thus been destroyed. But most of them have survived as recognisable geographical entities, either as the basis of a metropolitan district in the metropolitan counties, or as a whole non-metropolitan district in the rest of England.

Secondly, a boundary has been drawn around each of the largest urban areas of England — corresponding to the traditional conurbations outside Greater London — and these have been given a two-tier system of local government. These are the metropolitan counties, which are noteworthy both for their large populations and for the prominence of their lower-tier authorities, in terms of population size and of functional importance in the provision of services.

Thirdly, the lower-tier authorities in small town and rural England are in general much larger than their predecessors in the traditional structure. They are now also generally merged with a large urban area at the upper-tier level. In many areas this has meant a merging of different types of political system — the non- or semi-partisan with the fully partisan.

It is obvious in the short run that administrative reorganisations do not change socio-geographical factors as such and therefore the pattern of daily life is not significantly affected. But as the size of population of the authority increases, the average size of electoral area increases. This reduces the internal coherence of the ward, making it much more likely that it will not correspond to any recognisable social community. Thus the basis for a non-partisan system will be further weakened and an extension of party politics, both in geographical scope and in intensity, may be expected.

In addition, it is likely that urban political forms and styles will spread to the small towns and countryside. The increase in size of ward is one factor and it is reinforced by the fact that when political systems are merged, the one with the greater organising power will dominate. When partisan and non-partisan meet, the former usually but not invariably wins. Thus, party politics will become much more widespread in the local government system generally as well as in the large urban areas.

The above arguments all apply to all national political parties as such and do not distinguish between them in any way. The new system creates an environment favouring the success of political parties against independents generally, without indicating what sort of party system will result. The next step is to look at the factors helping to determine the nature of the party system in a local authority.

At present there is an asymmetry in the explanations that have been advanced to account for the type of party and the nature of the party system found in different localities. Quite different types of explanation are required to deal with the two major parties as opposed to the Liberals and such purely local parties as ratepayer and council tenants' parties.

Firstly, as might be expected from the general understanding of British politics, the relative strengths of Labour and Conservative are a reflection, not necessarily in a very straightforward way, of the social composition of the population. This can be shown by using any of the measures of social composition, for instance, occupational structure, housing conditions or class composition. None of these has any intrinsic superiority over the others, but they all point in the same direction.[21]

A more historical approach is needed to explain the presence of parties other than the two major ones. Many of the 'concealed' Conservative parties resulted from an anti-Labour alliance of Liberals and Conservatives which was a local response to the problems of electoral competition and which perhaps has continued as a distinct organisation

[21] F. R. Oliver and J. Stanyer, 'Some Aspects of the Financial Behaviour of County Boroughs', *Public Administration*, Summer 1969, pp. 169-84; D. S. Morris and K. Newton, 'Marginal Wards and Social Class', *British Journal of Political Science*, Oct 1971, pp. 503-7; W. P. Grant, 'Size of Place and Local Labour Strength', *British Journal of Political Science*, Apr 1972, pp. 259-60.

through inertial forces. An examination of Liberal candidatures in large authorities shows that it has the appearance of a stochastic process, which produces a scatter of interventions over time and across the ward system. A combination of factors may lead to Liberal successes at one point in time and a locking 'mechanism' may cause their role to persist. But in some urban areas the strength of the Liberals is something that has continued from the pre-war political system; in parts of Lancashire and Yorkshire, for instance, the Liberals have been traditionally successful. Ratepayer and other local parties are not generally found, or at least are not successful, in the large urban areas, the research suggests that the factors underlying the emergence and persistence of householder movements are relatively weak in British cities.[22]

In order to estimate the consequences of the new structure in the light of the logical model, it is first necessary to consider the Labour–Conservative two-party system and then to consider the chances of other parties, including the Liberals and Nationalists, maintaining the positions they have achieved in 1973 and 1974, both nationally and locally.

In many local political systems prior to the mid-1960s there was a great deal of *natural* continuity of council membership, created not by mechanical devices such as the aldermanic system or partial renewal, but by the existence of safe seats, advantages to incumbents, willingness to seek re-election and willingness to return after defeat. Indeed, it could be argued that in both partisan and non-partisan areas the inertial forces were so great that the adaptability of the system to the development or appearance of new values and new interests was reduced to a dangerously low level. Council composition may have reflected the social structure of previous decades.

The degree of continuity of a council's membership depends on a variety of factors that are not directly represented in the model, but also on the extent to which serving councillors are defeated. This latter factor is measured by the *national/local multiplier*. The greater the value of this multiplier, the greater the amount of change in a council's compo-

---

[22]   W. P. Grant, 'Independent Political Parties', Ph.D. thesis (Univ. of Exeter, 1973).

sition produced by any given range of variation in the relative support of the two parties. But for any given value of the multiplier the greater the variability of national support for the parties, the greater the changes in the composition of the council. These two factors are brought together in Table 1, which shows how they operate only in combination with each other.

TABLE 1
Range of National Support and the National/Local Multiplier

National/local multiplier

	1·0	2·0	3·0	4·0
	% of seats held by short-term members for stated NLM			
Range of national support for one party				
45 — 55	10	20	30	40
40 — 60	20	40	60	80
35 — 65	30	60	90	all
30 — 70	40	80	all	all

The above calculations assume that the locality is one in which the two parties are evenly balanced. In localities where one or other of the two is dominant the calculations at the extremes become more complicated.

For reasons that cannot be set out properly here, the greater the degree of partisanship in voting behaviour the greater the size of the multiplier. Intuitively it can be seen that if other factors grow in importance, this will weaken the relationship between the results of local elections and changes in national support for a political party. The question of the future variability of support for the national political parties, however, is more difficult to answer.

During the 1950s the fortunes of the two major parties did not appear to fluctuate very widely relative to each other and the consequence was that the membership of urban councils did not change rapidly. In those areas where there was a marked *national/local bias* in favour of one party this produced one-party systems, and commentators began to regard these as a permanent feature of some local political systems. But the period from 1967 onwards has been quite different; the trough into which the Labour Party sunk in the opinion polls of 1967-9 removed many of its long-serving members from the large urban councils and this was followed by a similar experience in 1971-2 for the Conservatives. Suddenly the notion of a one-party system needed revision and in many places control of local affairs was in the hands of relative newcomers to local government.[23]

The next step is to distinguish between *episodic* and *endemic* instability at the national level in the political system. Episodic instability occurs when a general state of relative stability in party fortunes is occasionally interrupted by a short period of instability, whilst endemic instability occurs when the situation of rapidly and widely varying fortunes continues for a long time.

Episodic instability is produced in three main ways: by a redistribution of seats, whether accompanied by structural reorganisation or not; by the rise and fall of a local political movement or a third party; and by a sudden change in political behaviour at the national level. In many parts of the country, from a detached point of view, such occurrences were welcome as a purgative, shaking out the older cohorts of members and facilitating the adaptation of the system to new forces and new interests. The combination of local government reorganisation and the changing pattern of party fortunes in the period 1967-74 will probably be seen in retrospect as a major phase in the evolution of the system of local democracy in Britain.

Episodic instability facilitates the change from one stable state to another, but suppose it is repeated at short intervals or continuously? A glance at Table 1 will show that the combination of a high national/local multiplier and wide changes in party support will produce councils with only small proportions of long-service members. This will be magnified in those areas with a substantial national/local bias; the minority party may find that it never has any long-service

[23]   The change is well illustrated in J. G. Bulpitt, *Party Politics in English Local Government* (London: Longmans, 1967). The county borough of Salford is classified as a one-party Labour system, yet shortly after the publication of the book the Conservatives took control.

members.[24]

The key factor in relating the outcomes of the electoral system to behaviour on the council is the process of socialisation *within* the council itself. What is therefore required is a model of socialisation generally which can be adapted to the special features of a local authority. Unfortunately there is no space here to present such a model, but the following analysis derives from a model of political socialisation developed by the present author.[25]

In this model, socialisation is regarded as one of the main factors in the maintenance of behavioural patterns over time and in the growth of consensus on procedural and substantive values. The form and extent of socialisation is strongly influenced by the degree of continuity of membership of the council. It argues that the longer people interact and the fewer the new participants entering in any given time-period, the greater the degree of consensus and the greater the inertial forces of the system.

If the greater political instability of the past seven years persists, then the processes of socialisation will be weakened on each council; members will tend to become short-term ones and at any given time there is likely to be a high proportion of newcomers.

Among the consequences of this must be counted the effects on council/officer relations. These are a particularly crucial and sensitive structural element in all British local government systems, and the traditional system depended on both socialising each other over a long period of time. The official needs effective and knowledgeable council members for the efficient discharge of his roles as usually conceived in these systems, and the council member needs sophisticated officers if he is to do likewise. The political boss in urban areas has been a pale shadow of his American counterpart; nevertheless, in many areas a number of council members

[24] Unfortunately there is insufficient space to spell out the detailed consequences of differing values of the national/local bias, or of the local support/seats won bias. But these concepts relate to a number of aspects of socialisation and control within a council. See Stanyer, in *Pol. Stud.*, June 1970, pp. 195 ff.

[25] J. Stanyer, 'A Theoretical Model of Political Socialisation', paper presented to the Conference on Political Socialisation, Exeter Univ. 1971.

have in the past created over a period of time a leadership role within council affairs and the local community. If the instability of political support at the national level continues in an extreme form, then such roles will be impossible to create in the future. Political leadership will be located outside the council.

Other consequences may be expected from a weakening of internal socialisation processes. Short-term councillors may cause more difficulty for citizens in the exercise of their representative roles, partly because they will be less well known and partly because of their lack of familiarity with the system. The council group may also be weakened in relation to the party outside, and this may be a source of greater tension between the two.

The model predicts, therefore, that natural continuity will be reduced in the new system, probably by a considerable amount, though this depends on the continuance of the recent pattern of national political behaviour. At the same time, mechanical continuity in the form of the aldermanic system and annual elections for some authorities has also been reduced. When natural continuity is high the arguments in favour of mechanical devices are fictitious, but, as has been shown above, there is some cause for concern about the future of many local authorities. The mechanism ought not to be an aldermanic system, for this has all sorts of odd side-effects, but both democracy and continuity could be ensured by some form of proportional representation which protects the minority in its bad years.

Members leave councils for reasons other than electoral defeat — death, resignation, disqualification, failure to seek re-election — and the model says nothing about these, nor can much be inferred about them in the new system. The chance for a former member, defeated or otherwise, to seek re-election, however, is a direct function of the frequency of elections. With quadrennial simultaneous retirement for some authorities, and a 'holiday' every fourth year in partial renewal systems, it is difficult not to believe that the loss of former council members between elections will be greater in the new system. Both the civic-conscious and the politically ambitious former members have many opportunities to serve the public interest or to further a political career outside the council chamber. If they become deeply concerned in these other activities they may be lost to the local government field.

The model of electoral behaviour predicts, therefore, a movement of power in urban politics away from the council chamber and committee room, partly towards the political organisations external to the council and partly towards official organisational structures. The key mechanism in these processes is socialisation, whose traditional role in local government will be greatly reduced. There are other relevant factors, but their force is not obviously so great as to counteract completely the effects of elections.

The present strength of the Liberals and Nationalists in British politics poses a different sort of problem. If they do not maintain their position in the immediate future then they will be seen in retrospect as another source of the episodic instability that has profoundly affected urban politics in the last decade. But if they remain at their present levels of support, then the model as it stands at the moment loses some of its usefulness. In those areas where the local party system is basically one of two-party competition, but where the parties are in fact say, Conservative and Liberal, or Labour and Nationalist, there is in principle no problem provided the relative national standing of the two parties that dominate the locality can be determined. The difficulty arises in multiparty systems at the local level. The model needs to be expanded to analyse behaviour in three-, four- or n-party situations. This will not be feasible until the theoretical foundations of the model are made more elaborate and systematic.

Urban electoral behaviour has thus been interpreted in this chapter as an intervening variable, linking the social processes of urban life and the national political scene with important aspects of behaviour within the urban local authority. The model thus performs the function required of it; it is 'end-on' to the analyses of other important social and political processes. Local elections in cities are restored, not to the same place as they were assigned in traditional local government 'theory' but to a central position as one of the linking mechanisms in urban political systems.

Variations in Service Provision: Politics at the Lay - Professional Interface

Janet Lewis

The techniques for statistical analysis of variations in service provision have been much further developed in England than abroad. In the United States the preoccupations have not been to trace the determinants of variations in service provision, as Bleddyn Davies has done, but to examine the relationship between socio-economic characteristics and forms of government on the one hand, and service provision on the other. For the United States studies some variant of the following model appears to have been used.[1]

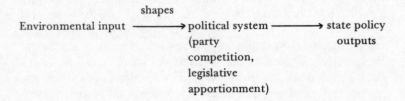

There has been considerable debate about which factors within the political system might be significant, and a number of studied have also suggested that environmental factors alone affect policy outputs. The current view seems to be that factors within the political system can be important, and attempts have been made to extend the above model by including such variables as political culture, professionalism,

[1] This operative model was proposed by R. Weber and W. Shaffer, 'Public Opinion and American State Policy Making', *Midwest Journal of Political Science,* Nov 1972, p. 683.

party competition, regional and state differences, and so on.[2] Policy outputs have also been differentiated in order to make the model more sensitive, either by dividing expenditure into component services (comparing welfare and education expenditure with that on highways and natural resources) or by taking such other indicators of output as the enactment of certain kinds of legislation in different states.[3] However, none of these studies has led to an exposition of the ways in which the variables, particularly those within the political system, interact, and such an exposition will be the focus of this essay. I hope that in discussing the processes involved within the context of the community and the services provided, I shall clarify some of the relationships and raise some issues for further discussion and research.

In order simply to structure the discussion, I should like to put forward a 'model' of the relationship between input and

[2] The original works which stressed the importance of socio-economic rather than political variables were those of Richard E. Dawson and James A. Robinson, 'Inter-party Competition, Economic Variables, and Welfare Policies in the American States', *Journal of Politics*, May 1963, pp. 265-89; Richard I. Hofferbert, 'The Relation between Public Policy and some Structural and Environmental Variables in the American States', *American Political Science Review*, Mar 1966, pp. 73-82; and Thomas R. Dye, *Politics, Economics and the Public: Policy Outcomes in the American States* (Chicago: Rand McNally, 1966). These studies have been criticised for a number of reasons; see, for example, H. Jacob and M. Lipsky, 'Output, Structures and Power: An Assessment of Changes in the Study of State and Local Politics', *Journal of Politics*, May 1968, pp. 510-38. Articles which have attempted to extend the model include C. Cnudde and D. McCrone, 'Party Competition and Welfare Policies in the American States', *American Political Science Review*, Sep 1969, pp. 858-66; and a number of articles by Sharkansky, including I. Sharkansky and Richard I. Hofferbert, 'Dimensions of State Politics, Economics and Public Policy', *American Political Science Review*, Sep 1969, pp. 867-79; M. Hoffman and J. Prather, 'The Independent Effect of Region on State Government Expenditure', *Social Science Quarterly*, June 1972, pp. 52-65; and numerous others.

[3] See especially Sharkansky and Hofferbert, in *Amer. Pol. Sci. Rev.*, Sep 1969, pp. 867-79; and Weber and Shaffer, in *Midwest J. Pol. Sci.*, Nov 1972, p. 683.

service provision, the component parts of which will then be
discussed in turn. The model has been derived from some
work on social service provision carried out in four London
boroughs and many of the ideas discussed arose during the
course of this research. However, they have not been tested
on a wider scale and therefore must be treated as informed
speculation rather than validated interpretation.

Before discussing in more detail each part of Fig. 1, a word
about problems of definition seems appropriate. Two terms
in this field raise considerable problems of meaning for they
are used frequently and often in contradictory ways. The
first is *output* and the second *policy;* the two are often
combined so that we also have 'policy outputs' in addition to
'policy outcomes' and 'policy impacts'. 'Output' may be
defined as the 'product of any industry or exertion viewed
quantitatively; the result given to the world',[4] and in manu-
facturing or process industry 'output' — the total product —
is comparatively easy to identify or measure. However, in the
case of service industries this is much more difficult; is the
product to be conceived of in terms of the services provided
or the effect these services have on the population? In other
words, are the products of local authorities to be taken as the
number of new homes, clinics or schools which are built, or
are we concerned with assessing the changes in the circumstances of the population served? A true measure of 'output'
would be a measure of the latter, but techniques to do this
are still in their infancy.[5] As a substitute, therefore, researchers have concentrated on service provision; for example,
the number of people in residential homes, which is a measure of 'throughput', or upon service expenditure per head of
population, a true measure of *input.* If output measures do
not exist it may be necessary to use figures which are available as indicators of outputs, but many researchers have
failed to demonstrate that they realise the distinction and
appear to take expenditure as a direct measure of 'output'. It
is likely that this confusion over the term *output* has also led

4   The *Oxford English Dictionary.*
5   For a discussion of output measurement, see Alan Williams, 'Eco-
    nomic Analysis and the Ten Year Plan', *Clearing House for Local
    Authority Social Services Research,* no. 1 (Univ. of Birmingham,
    1973) pp. 36-7.

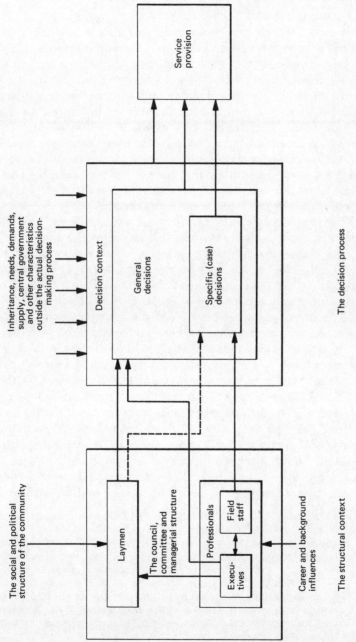

Fig. 1 The structure and process of service provision in local government

to a proliferation of other terms such as 'policy impact' and 'outcome' which have been used to indicate the effect that services have on the population. A standardisation of terminology would be of great benefit to all concerned.

As input figures like expenditure are clearly a very crude measure of service provision, we must find better measures of assessing the true output of urban services before we can talk about the effectiveness of urban decision-making. This requires a study of the relationship between services provided and their effectiveness, but if we are also interested in developing ways of introducing the 'better' services once we know what they are, we need to be concerned with examining the factors which affect decisions about services.

In the absence of measures of effectiveness, political scientists and sociologists can still examine the community political systems and their relationship with service provision; it is this area which will be discussed here, with the consequence that the term 'output' will be avoided and I shall be concerned with service provision rather than effectiveness.

The use of the word *policy* will similarly be avoided where possible because here again there are considerable variations in usage. In some cases it is used to indicate the sum of the decisions and non-decisions taken in a particular area so that it is the 'pattern of resources' committed to that area.[6] Other writers have used 'policy' to refer to norms, to definitions of objectives, to the priorities set, to plans and to 'decision rules'.[7] While it is quite possible to take one of these definitions and talk about 'policy' on that basis, it seems preferable to talk about norms, objectives and priorities as such. In addition, it is often difficult to distinguish between something that is merely a 'decision', and something which is

[6]   J. Dearlove, *The Politics of Policy in Local Government* (Cambridge: Cambridge Univ. Press, 1973) p. 2.

[7]   Chester Barnard, in 'Comments on the Job of the Executive', *Harvard Business Review*, Spring 1940, pp. 295-308, gives twelve meanings of the word 'policy'. The concept has also been discussed by Sir Geoffrey Vickers in *The Art of Judgement* (London: Chapman & Hall, 1965), but it is Desmond Keeling's book *Management in Government* (London: Allen & Unwin, 1972) which offers the alternatives which seem particularly appropriate to local government.

'policy'. These different attributes will therefore be kept separate in this essay, and as far as possible the focus will be on decisions.

I turn now to elaborate the processes involved in decision-making in English local government as represented in Fig. 1. Those components which have been studied most will be discussed first and an attempt will then be made to look at the relationship between the components of the process. The structure of this essay is therefore to look briefly at the laymen and the professionals as distinct groups and at their positions in the local government structure. The formal decision-making procedure will then be examined along with the constraints and other external forces which affect this: inheritance, needs, demands, and central government influences. The essay will conclude with a discussion of the interaction of the groups of laymen and professionals and the way their attributes and interactions affect the decision-making process.

THE STRUCTURAL CONTEXT

The laymen

The laymen sit on the council and its committees; they consist of a group of elected councillors with the addition until recently of a fixed proportion of aldermen selected by the councillors. The term 'laymen' in this context indicates the status which this group of individuals holds in the local authority structure. Many are 'professionals' in their own right, working as lawyers, teachers, accountants or businessmen. However, as members of the council they represent the views of the community rather than being expected to have access to expert knowledge. This 'layman's' position is exemplified by the voluntary, part-time nature of the activity, plus the lack of systematic training for the work, so that in almost all cases laymen cannot hope to compete with the paid officials in questions requiring detailed knowledge.

The position of laymen can be examined from two points of view: the characteristics of the individuals who make up the council, or the characteristics of the councils themselves and their corporate identity. Considering the councillors

themselves first, we know that in a number of respects councillors differ quite markedly from the general population.
They are older, fewer of them are women, but more of them
come from high social class groups and have received higher
levels of education.[8] However, we do not know whether
these differences are distributed evenly between councils
throughout the country or whether certain kinds of communities elect very different kinds of representatives. The
role of the councillor has been discussed frequently and a
number of different classifications suggested which can be
found in the literature.[9] No attempts have yet been made to
relate role differences to service provision generally, or to
examine whether there is a relationship between community
characteristics and roles taken by councillors on the corresponding council.

Looking at councils rather than councillors, we know that
the political complexion of councils varies and that although
elections can result in changes of party control, there is a
broad relationship between the social class of an area and the
party affiliation of its local council. However, if one is
interested in a more sophisticated analysis of the party structure, such as that proposed by Bulpitt, who made a distinction between one- and two-party systems and divisions within
these,[10] there is no systematic evidence available on the
relationship between the characteristics of the community
and the party system of the council. There may not be a
relationship, but if there is it could be a useful variable in
explaining service differences.

In addition to their party structure, local councils can vary
in their formal authority structure. This is because the
essence of local authority activity in England and Wales is

8   Committee on the Management of Local Government, vol. II: *The
    Local Government Councillor* (London: H.M.S.O., 1967).
9   See, for example, Hugh Heclo, 'The Councillor's Job', *Public
    Administration*, Summer 1969, pp. 185-202; G. W. Jones, 'The
    Functions and Organisation of Councillors', *Public Administra-
    tion*, Summer 1973, pp. 135-46; and K. Newton, 'Links between
    Leaders and Citizens in a Local Political System', *Policy and Poli-
    tics*, June 1973, pp. 287-305.
10 J. G. Bulpitt, *Party Politics in English Local Government* (London:
    Longmans, 1967).

'government by committee', and the ways in which committees are co-ordinated and controlled can vary considerably.[11] Traditionally, committees within the limits laid down by the council's standing orders have had considerable autonomy, subject to council approval. However, with the increasing complexity and quantity of servies provided have come suggestions that the activites of committees should be co-ordinated and that there should be more positive planning of local authority services as a whole. From the council point of view, this has usually resulted in the formation of a 'policy committee' whose job has been to decide priorities between services and to co-ordinate the work of different committees. The extent to which these committees have actually been appointed, and the degree to which they are able to make a positive contribution to planning, varies between authorities. Some councils have no such committees and they exist in other authorities in name only. Thus some councils have a relatively centralised committee structure or decision-making system while others, where a policy committee does not exist and informal mechanisms for co-ordination are also absent, retain autonomous committees and a decentralised decision-making structure. Here again the relationships between the different council structures and either the community or the services provided have not been explored in any way. There is therefore very little known about the importance of councillor and council differences in the decision-making process.

The professionals

The day-to-day administration of the services is carried on within the departments of local authorities, each the responsibility of a chief officer and, depending on the service, containing a considerable number of people of different ranks who are concerned with planning and running the particular services. It is not appropriate here to go into a discussion of the number of people in a department who are

[11] For a discussion of committees in local government, see Peter G. Richards, *The New Local Government System* (London: Allen & Unwin, 1968) pp. 103-13; and K. C. Wheare, *Government by Committee* (Oxford: Clarendon Press, 1955) chap. 7.

'professionals' in the strict definition of the term, it being sufficient to say that many people employed in the services have had considerable training, could carry out their specialised activities autonomously and are employed full-time by the local authority in what is seen as a 'professional capacity'. This being the case, they will be referred to as 'professionals' during the course of this discussion.

The structure of the departmental and consequently managerial component of local authority activity has been the focus of considerable discussion in recent years, some of it arising from the discussion mentioned above which considered the role of the elected member in planning and co-ordinating services, but also resulting from the spread of the 'managerial revolution' into local government. As with the committee structure, the departments have traditionally been relatively independent and there has been little co-ordinated planning of services. Times are changing! The Town Clerk is becoming the Chief Executive, chief officers are beginning to work together as a 'management team', and the introduction of P.P.B.S. and other management techniques has encouraged co-ordinated planning. However, this movement is gradual and its spread uneven so that there is still considerable variation between authorities. Members of the Institute of Local Government studies have charted the distribution of various kinds of management structure;[12] for example, the presence of a federal, integral or separatist structure based on whether an authority has attributes including a principal officer, a management team of officers and a policy committee. Of the 89 authorities examined they found that only 12 had an integrated structure, so the pace of change is still quite slow.[13]

[12]   Publications include R. Greenwood, A. Norton and J. D. Stewart, 'Recent Changes in the Internal Organisation of County Boroughs: I. Committees; II. Delegation and Departmental reorganisation', *Public Administration*, Summer and Autumn 1969, pp. 151-67, 289-306.

[13]   R. Greenwood and J. D. Stewart, 'Towards a Typology of English Local Government', *Political Studies*, Mar 1973, pp. 64-9. The slowness in the introduction of corporate planning techniques is confirmed by R. C. Lucking, K. Howard and M. J. Greenwood, 'Corporate Planning and Management', *Town Planning Review*, Apr 1974, pp. 131-45.

Some advocates of managerial reform assume that changes in the structure will automatically improve service provision. Unfortunately this is an unwarranted assumption in that these studies of managerial and structural differences within local government, although becoming more sophisticated,[14] have not as yet been extended to an examination of the services provided. It is quite possible that the managerial structure of the authority as a whole is a relatively unimportant factor if we are concerned with what decisions are actually taken. A number of writers have stressed the importance of 'style' as opposed to structure. John Stewart of INLOGOV has himself suggested that local government requires a 'learning style' rather than a static style as at present, but he has not incorporated these concepts into a systematic study.[15] Keeling distinguishes between an 'administrative' and a 'managerial' style,[16] the emphasis either being positive and towards expansion and risk-taking, or aimed at preserving the *status quo*. The causal importance of style has not yet been tested, nor has the relationship between style and structure been explored; one can hypothesise that style rather than structure is the more important factor in explaining differences in service provision.

THE DECISION PROCESS

Before going on to examine the vital though nebulous interaction between the laymen and the professionals, I want first to discuss the more specific aspects of decision-making. It is quite clear that within the local authority structure the formal decisions taken in committee by the councillors with officer advice play an important part in the process of providing services for the community. Outside influences are also

---

[14] See, for example, R. Greenwood and C. R. Hinings, 'The Comparative Study of Local Government Organisation, 1972-76', *Policy and Politics*, Mar 1973, pp. 213-21; R. Greenwood and J. D. Stewart, 'Corporate Planning and Management Organisation', *Local Government Studies*, Oct 1972, pp. 25-40.

[15] J. D. Stewart, *Management in Local Government: A Viewpoint* (London: Charles Knight, 1971) p. 33.

[16] Keeling, *Management in Government*, chap. 5.

at work and these will be touched on later, but the committee decisions are particularly vital when considering service development. The pressures to prevent change can of course be quite considerable: projects, plans or services can be stopped or prevented from happening for a number of different reasons including lack of money, lack of enthusiasm on the part of some councillor or officer, and various forces outside the control of the council. However, if positive action or change is to be introduced, it has to be accepted and approved by the committee as a first step in its progress towards implementation.

The process of interaction which is discussed in later sections of this essay is of great importance to an understanding of what goes on and what gets decided, but it is also necessary to recognise the formal procedures that are gone through; the committee is only one stage in what happens and it is necessary to make some distinction between the decisions taken by the committee and those taken by other actors. This is not to suggest that all committees take decisions on a similar range of matters, nor that all important decisions are taken within the committee: many are taken beforehand in party caucus meetings, but even these decisions are ratified by the committee before their implementation.

As a rule of thumb one can suggest that any general decisions taken about the direction of the service, the stated goals or the recognised norms, and any planning decisions, are initially taken or ratified by the committee. At the other end of the spectrum, decisions about individual cases — for example, the allocation of council houses or the admission of an elderly person to sheltered accommodation — are generally not decided in committee, but by the member of staff dealing with the case. In between the decisions taken at either end of this continuum are a whole host of decisions which are difficult to categorise. Those which are customarily submitted to committee for formal approval involve specific cases where precedents are being set and committee 'decision rules' thereby made, as well as numerous routine administrative decisions about buildings, regulations and staff matters which are neither general decisions nor decision rules.

It is important to stress that not all service-related decisions are taken in committee, and even where a range of decisions can be identified as being customarily the concern of the committee, these decisions have by no means a *direct* relationship with service provision. Other factors intervene or create very different circumstances in which the decisions are taken and the services provided. These external influences and constraints are of some causal importance for variations in service provision, and it is to them that I now turn.

External factors and constraints in the decision-making process

(i) *Inheritance*. A local authority at any one point in time is operating within the constraints of a pattern of provision inherited from a previous time-period. The possible rate of expansion or contraction is constrained by the existing provision, for it is difficult to reduce actual provision significantly (as distinct from plans), while resources to enable rapid changes to be introduced are often lacking. Thus, when assessing service provision and looking for explanations or variation it is necessary to take into account that a considerable part of what services exist have not arisen from decisions taken by the current political 'regime'; the regime of five years previously or even earlier might be more important.[17]

(ii) *Needs*. Recent studies have found little relationship between indices of need on the one hand and service provision on the other.[18] If the analysis of the essay is in any way correct, one would not expect to find direct relation-

[17] For example, B. P. Davies, in *Social Needs and Resources* (London: Michael Joseph, 1968) p. 156, said: 'There is a high degree of correlation between identical indices taken in widely different years, the correlations being high enough to show a pattern of provision in 1952 correlated with that planned for 1974.'

[18] J. Packman, *Child Care: Needs and Numbers* (London: Allen & Unwin, 1968); N. Boaden, *Urban Policy-making: Influences on County Boroughs in England and Wales* (Cambridge: Cambridge Univ. Press, 1971). However, for a causal analysis of the determinants of variations in performance, including needs, see B. P. Davies et al. *Variations in services for the aged* (London: G. Bell and Sons, 1971) and *Variations in children's services among British urban authorities* (London: G. Bell and Sons, 1972).

ships; there are too many intervening variables for this to be possible. However, this is not to say that 'need' plays no part. The concept of need is difficult to define and the number of people 'in need' varies according to the definition chosen, but on any one definition the number of needy people varies between different areas.[19] It is likely that these varying amounts of 'need' will put different amounts of pressure on to the services and this in turn will affect the perception the officers and councillors have of the desirability of providing services. We know very little about the relationship between 'need', however it is defined, and pressure on the services, or about the way in which needs are perceived by laymen and professionals. However, it does seem that one component of differences in service provision may be due to differences in 'need'.

(iii) *Demands.* Not only do needs and perceptions vary between areas, but the take-up of services is not necessarily uniform across the country, or between social classes.[20] Therefore when looking at figures of social service provision — the hours worked by home helps, the number of people in residential accommodation, and so on — some of the variations found can be attributed to differences in the service actually provided, but some may be the result of differences in the active demand for that service, a factor which is outside the control of the council and the management of the local authority.

In addition to differential take-up of the services offered, demands can also affect the amount of a service provided in that, at the margin at least, there are other bodies which can make or withhold demands on local authorities. Police referral patterns, expansionist demands from pressure groups and private-sector substitute services, among other things, can result in local authorities facing very different patterns of demand in areas which could be thought to be similar in other ways.

[19]   The work done by the Government Social Survey would seem to indicate this: see particularly Amelia Harris, *Social Welfare for the Elderly* (London: H.M.S.O., 1968).

[20]   See, for example, from a slightly different context, M. L. Johnson, 'Self-perception of Need amongst the Elderly: An Analysis of Illness Behaviour', *Sociological Review*, Nov 1972, pp. 521-31.

(iv) *Supply*. If one assumes that figures of service provision in some way reflect the intentions of those involved in the decision-making process, then it is quite clear that not only do needs, demands and inheritance independently affect these figures, but so also in the short term do problems of supply. There are shortages of many categories of trained staff in local authority work, and even if ·authorities are anxious to expand services and increase their establishment accordingly, they may be quite unable to fill these posts. In some circumstances variations in supply are due to a 'good officer — good authority' syndrome in which the popular employers attract high-calibre staff, while the authorities which restrict the activities of their workers or do not offer conditions for 'professional' work fail to fill their job vacancies. Supply problems may therefore be more elastic than some employers suggest, but it is certainly true that, in the short term, supply difficulties can prevent the intentions of expansionist committees being realised.

(v) *Central government*. Through its control of loan sanction, central government has a considerable influence over local government activity, although mainly in the negative sense in that it can withhold its consent. A local authority can apply for loan sanction for a particular project and be refused on the basis that other authorities should have preference, or that it is not government policy to encourage buildings of that kind. Thus again, figures of service provision cannot indicate committee intention.[21]

(vi) *Case decisions*. It was mentioned in the earlier section

---

[21] Central government can also make positive suggestions for local authority activity through the use of circulars. These are not discussed here as they do not act as constraints in the same way, but it is worth pointing out that these circulars do not automatically produce the action which central government would like. The way in which information and advice from circulars is treated is in many ways a good indication of the style and orientation of the authorities and deserves a separate study in itself. Evidence from my study suggests that circulars in local government can meet similar reactions to National Health Service circulars as discussed in Rosemary Stewart and Janet Sleeman, *Continuously under Review*, Occasional Paper on Social Administration No. 20 (London: Bell, 1967).

that many specific decisions about particular individuals are taken by the case worker or other staff member dealing with the case. Very little is known about the factors which influence the decisions taken in the face-to-face context, but there are evidently considerable differences between individuals.[22] This means that whatever decisions are taken at the committee level about the overall direction of the services and the priorities and norms, we have no reason to suppose that case decisions are automatically made to fit in with the committee's views.

The conclusion of this section reaffirms what was said above: that, owing to the intervention of these external factors, it is impossible to make inferences about the nature of the decision-making process from service provision statistics. Few of these external factors have been studied systematically to date, but nor have the interactions between the laymen and the professionals, and it is this which forms the focus of the remainder of the essay.

THE RELATIONSHIP BETWEEN THE LAYMEN AND THE PROFESSIONALS

The absence in England of any systematic studies which have examined the interaction between the councillors and the officers at the committee level is remarkable. A number of case studies have been conducted but they have not led to the formulation of general hypotheses about the relationship

---

[22] Training among other things appears to affect decisions taken: see E. M. Goldberg, *Helping the Aged* (London: Allen & Unwin, 1970) p. 192; and A. Rosen and D. Lieberman, 'The Experimental Evaluation of Interview Performance of Social Workers', *Social Service Review*, Sep 1972, pp. 395-412. But so does the practice of the department in which individuals work; see J. Heywood and B. Allen, *Financial Help in Social Work* (Manchester: Manchester Univ. Press, 1971); and V. George, *Foster Care: Theory and Practice* (London: Routledge & Kegan Paul, 1970) p. 227. The effect of personality differences seems unexplored.

between these two groups.[23] Most writing therefore falls back on the hoary cliche 'Councillors decide policy, officers administer it', although this distinction has been demonstrated to be logically untenable.[24] It is worth examining this in a little more detail.

Although city managers in the United States and departmental chief officers in England have different responsibilities, their positions in relation to their elected members would seem to be similar. The findings of Ronald Loveridge in *City Managers in Legislative Politics* can therefore be seen to have relevance to the British experience and suggest a useful model. Loveridge found that three-quarters of his managers rejected the policy — administration dichotomy and felt that they were also concerned with policy, although nine-tenths of the councilmen in the same cities still endorsed the distinction and thought of the manager as an administrator. The managers were clearly shown to be involved in 'policy-making' which resulted in role-conflict for the managers: should they adopt an executive orientation in keeping with their training, function and circumstances, or should they act according to the expectation of the councilmen? Loveridge suggests that

> The result is an *ad hoc*, uncertain game of policy advocacy, played out in the very person executive — legislative exchanges of council — manager politics in which the councilmen have the formal authority, but the manager

---

[23]   Studies include David Peschek and J. Brand, *Policies and Politics in Secondary Education*, Greater London Papers No. II, (London: London School of Economics, 1966); A. Brier, 'The Decision Process in Local Government: A Case Study of Fluoridation in Hull', *Public Administration*, Summer 1970, pp. 153-68; and R. Saran, *Policy-making in Secondary Education* (London: Oxford Univ. Press, 1973).

[24]   See the report of the oral evidence of D. N. Chester and Professor Griffith to the Committee on the Management of Local Government, vol. I, para. 109.

can use a number of strategies to shape the decisions taken.[25]

The strategies discussed will be familiar to anyone who has worked in local government: the general strategies of the development of information and the need for appropriate timing, private behind-the-scenes persuasion, 'education' of the council and the development of trust. More specifically, a United States city manager can propose changes through the budget, through authorising a formal report, employing an outside consulting firm to make recommendations, by using his discretion in the preparation of the council agenda, or by mobilising community forces to support changes.

In England councillors also tend to use the distinction between policy and administration and insist that the officers administer; thus the officer is likely to be in a similar position of role-conflict. No one can dispute that the councillors on committees and councils *take* the final decisions, but the tendency is to equate this decision-taking with 'policy-making' and to suggest that because the officer is not involved in these final decisions, he is not involved in policy-making. This ignores the fact that the processes leading up to the decision are very much the concern of the officers, including the initiation of new ideas and many other broader aspects of planning and providing a service. From this wider perspective officers can be seen to be centrally involved in the process of providing services.

It is therefore impossible to draw a sharp division between the functions of councillors and officers, for as Kramer has said in discussing the relationship between board members (equivalent in status to councillors) and executives (officers) in voluntary agencies for social welfare:

> While both are theoretically involved in policy formulation, the board alone has the right to adopt policy and the executive is directly responsible for its implementation ... it may be observed that the board's policy adoption powers can be ... called ... 'the illusion of final

[25]   Ronald O. Loveridge, *City Managers in Legislative Politics* (Indianapolis: Bobbs-Merrill, 1971) p. 142.

authority', since in administering and implementing policy decisions the executive can affect their outcome and may therefore have the last word. Furthermore, it may be said that the executive, because of his skill and closer identification with the agency, tends more often to be the initiator and actually controls the process of policy formulation. His influence is manifested not only in the selection of particular issues but also in the presentation of information regarding the likely outcomes of alternative proposals presented to the board.[26]

It would seem to be useful to conceptualise the relationship between the two groups as one of *negotiation*[27] or, as Kramer has also suggested, of *exchange*. If this view of the relationship is accepted, further research is needed to discover what kinds of negotiation take place, what strategies are used by either side, and whether there are systematic differences between councils, individual councillors or officers in 'the rules of the game'.

Attitudes and values

This essay has so far dealt with the form and structure of lay — professional relationships and said very little about their content. This is an area of considerable importance to an understanding both of the services themselves and such matters as the structure and style of an authority. Lay — professional negotiations or exchanges on matters of service development occur within the context of widely varying stated and unstated views of people and of the world. Research has often focused upon 'policy-making' or 'decision-taking'; we know little of the world-views of councillors and officers in so far as they operate in the broader aspects of service development. Perhaps this neglect is due in part to the limitations of the 'mental models' of local govern-

---

[26] R. M. Kramer, 'Ideology, Status and Power in Board — Executive Relationships', *Social Work*, Oct 1965, p. 113.

[27] It has also been suggested that the interactions of different professional groups are governed by a process of negotiation; see A. Strauss *et al. Psychiatric Ideologies and Institutions* (New York: Free Press of Glencoe, 1964) chap. 15.

ment held by academic commentators and practitioners alike.

On the one hand there is the model of local government as 'local democracy' and representation. Here the focus is on the election of councillors and their activities once they are councillors: ward representative, party activist and committee member, policy-maker, or ombudsman. In this context, the services to which attention is paid are those which affect the community (refuse collection or uneven paving-stones, for example), even though they constitute only a small part of local activity, or those with a high political content, predominantly certain aspects of housing and education.[28] The councillors themselves often seem to hold this view of local government, as do many political scientists. On the other hand the alternative model sees local government as the provider of services, a position adhered to by many administrators both practising and academic. This view tends to emphasise the decisions taken by professionals rather than by the authority as a whole, and as a consequence ignores both the contributions made by councillors and the influence of the political context within which local government is set.

It is perhaps due to the lack of overlap of these two models that so few attempts have been made to link the activities of the representative elements of local authorities with their functions of providing services. An exploration of the models of local government would seem to be an area of enormous interest. At the same time, it is possible to identify some of the various attitudes which could play a part in determining the specific services which are provided. Some of these attitudes apply particularly to councillors and some to both officers and councillors, but for the sake of brevity the distinction will not be made here, the supposition being that individuals within both groups may hold these views.

(i) *The scope of government and the 'rate'.* A particularly relevant concept is what has been called 'the scope of govern-

28 It is services in these terms which are discussed by political scientists: for instance, Bulpitt, *Party Politics in English Local Government;* and H. V. Wiseman, *Local Government at Work* (London: Routledge & Kegan Paul, 1967).

ment': what activities individuals consider it appropriate for local government to perform. Generally, councillor attitudes run along a continuum from government as properly a provider of minimal services to an all-embracing view of government responsibility. Councillors in Kensington did not consider that the council should take over what they saw as the preserve of private enterprise, and felt services to be better provided by voluntary agencies than by the council.[29]

Allied to this attitude or perhaps a component part of it are attitudes to money. A local council raises money from its community by fixing a 'rate', and it is in the process of rate determination that the alternatives of providing or not providing a service are brought out most clearly. Some councils seem relatively unconcerned about rate levels, and if the services are felt to be needed then the money has to be raised, whereas other councils are impressed more by the need to be seen to be keeping the rate down than providing particular levels of service.

(ii) *The deserving and the undeserving.* Apart from general views about providing services, there are also very significant attitudes towards people who ask for help, or who otherwise receive services. The traditional English distinction between the deserving and the undeserving poor would appear to be alive and well, with the kind of service offered depending as much on the donor's perception of how the recipient reached the position of needing help as on the kind of help requested.[30] Titmuss has discussed the increasing amount of 'dependence' created by industrial society[31] and it would seem that certain categories of 'dependence' evoke much warmer feelings than others. The elderly are not criticised when they retire and a wide range of services are provided for them with community approval; doing things

---

[29] See Dearlove, *The Politics of Policy in Local Government*, chap. 10.

[30] Heywood and Allen, *Financial Help in Social Work;* G. Smith and R. Harris, 'Ideologies of Need and the Organisation of Social Work Departments', *British Journal of Social Work*, Spring 1972, pp. 27-45.

[31] Richard M. Titmuss, *Essays on 'the Welfare State'*, 2nd ed. (London: Allen & Unwin, 1963) chap. 2.

for 'the old folk' is a widely expressed sentiment. Similarly, children appear to be considered innocents for whom help should be unquestioningly provided if it is needed. Working-age adult clients, on the other hand, can be seen either within a context in which they are deviants — 'scroungers' or 'lay-abouts' who are trying to 'exploit society' — or as people who in difficult situations need help. Faced with a homeless family, a drug addict, an alcoholic or someone mentally ill, the response of the authority can either be a punitive one of providing a deterrent or no support at all, or it can be a therapeutic one offering what assistance is available.

These variations, though largely unexplored, are perhaps vested in varying perceptions of the mainsprings of human behaviour. Such varying views among decision-makers clearly have an effect on the services provided, leading in some areas to a concentration of support on the elderly and children and other 'legitimate dependent' groups, and in the other areas to wide-ranging, non-punitive support services for clients who would be considered 'deviants' elsewhere. Therefore attitudes affect not just the role of government in service provision and the amount of money spent, but also what the money is spent on.

(iii) *Professionalism.* A separate but possibly related question is one of professionalism and professional legiti-macy. It was clear in my study of health and social service provision that the councillors on one council made a sharp distinction between the competence of their medical staff and their social workers. This could not have been due to the lack of formal qualifications of the latter group and seemed to result from a basic lack of trust, stemming in part from the different views of clients mentioned above. The councillors considered that homeless families were 'wasting public money', 'had got themselves into these difficulties by not paying the rent', and that to help them would be 'to en-courage others' to act in a similar fashion. They considered that the social workers were much too 'soft' and were 'taken in' by the families concerned. In these circumstances the councillors were not prepared to delegate as much respon-sibility to social workers, particularly in cases where money was involved, as they were to doctors employed by the council. These councillors were much more suspicious of the social workers than in other authorities, and although it is difficult to trace the way this lack of trust affected the service provided by the social workers themselves, professional morale seemed lower.

While these attitudes and values can be seen to be distinct from each other, they could be thought to have a common denominator in social class. Very little work has been done in examining the attitudes of different social classes to local government and its services, but in relation to the attitudes discussed above, middle-class Conservatives are considered to be committed to minimal government and keeping the rate down, whereas working-class Labour Party supporters are thought to favour the expansion of the scope of government and are prepared to spend money to achieve this. However, in relation to attitudes towards recipients of help and to professionals, the 'authoritarianism' of many working-class people[32] suggests that councils on which they predominated would tend to be punitive towards minority groups, and suspicious of those who hold alternative definitions of reality to themselves, namely many social workers. On the other hand, traditional Conservative attitudes towards clients have been to stress the need for individual independence and hence minimal provision of services, but it is not known what attitudes towards social workers they might hold.

These are clearly very crude distinctions and it is not known to what extent stereotyped views are related to attitudes held by individuals. These are also the attitudes of the extremes and there are large groups of people who do not fit into either category, such as the 'middle-class radicals,'[33] or, on Eysenck's definition, the 'tender-minded' of either the

[32] See S. M. Lipset, *Political Man* (New York: Doubleday, 1960) chap. 3; for a discussion (but not an adequate refutation) of his view, see S. Miller and F. Reissman, 'Working Class Authoritarianism: A Critique of Lipset', *British Journal of Sociology*, Sep 1961, pp. 263-76. See also M. Kohn, *Class and Conformity* (Homewood, Ill.: Dorsey Press, 1969); and H. Gabennesch, 'Authoritarianism as World View', *American Journal of Sociology*, Mar 1972, pp. 857-75.

[33] See Frank Parkin, *Middle Class Radicalism* (Manchester: Manchester Univ. Press, 1968).

right or the left[34] (members of the Bow Group and the
Fabian Society, for example). It is possible therefore that
there are a considerable number of individuals who, for
reasons in their personal history, support the Conservative or
the Labour Party but who hold very similar views. It seems
likely that it will be from a group such as this that individuals
who support the idea of a broad scope of government and a
consequently high 'rate', coupled with a therapeutic stance
towards the underprivileged and support for social workers,
will come. These are testable propositions rather than 'hard'
findings, but this is an area which it would seem most rewarding to explore.

PARTY SYSTEMS AND ACTOR ORIENTATIONS

Previous sections have emphasised the negotiated aspects of
the relationship between laymen and professionals and the
extent to which the attitudes held by both groups, towards
clients and each other, can influence service provision. This
leads one to ask whether there are systematic patternings of
attitudes and relationships between these groups, and if so on
what basis.

The relationship between the two groups of councillor and
officer may be conflictual or consensual. If one accepts that
most people dislike conflict in their work and that officers
are relatively free to move as jobs are plentiful, it seems
plausible to suggest that officers will gravitate towards areas
where they find their work relatively congenial. Given also
that there are many authorities which never experience a
change of political party (although there can also be 'regime'
change in one-party systems as a result of different factions
alternating in control), it seems likely that the most prevalent
relationship will be that of consensus between stable political
regimes and long-serving officers. This consensus will result in
authorities reaching an equilibrium state in which there is
agreement on such matters as the appropriate rate of change
and the proper scope of government.

If most authorities are in an equilibrium state, it is then

---

[34]   H. J. Eysenck, *The Psychology of Politics* (London: Routledge &
Kegan Paul, 1954).

necessary to ask in what circumstances there will be consensus on the need for service development as opposed to a continuation of the *status quo,* and in what circumstances the equilibrium will be upset. In the latter case, this is clearly most likely to happen within two-party systems: the new majority party after an election can take a fresh look at priorities and plans and often bring a new perspective to existing services. In some authorities this could result in conflict between the councillors and the officers, but in most places officers will be sufficiently flexible to cope with the relatively minor changes made and a new equilibrium will be reached. However, I would also suggest that the circumstances in which there is agreement between the lay and professional groups on the desirability of developing services are more likely to occur in two-party rather than one-party systems.

This suggestion rests on the belief that there are differences in the motivation of people standing for different kinds of councils and in the way they view the work required when they become councillors. Fenton has suggested two categories of 'issue-oriented' and 'job-oriented' councilmen,[35] the former being councillors who are motivated by a desire to achieve specific service aims, and the latter where the attributes of the position, prestige, desire to serve the community generally and the formal and procedural aspects are the major attraction. Fenton found a relationship between issue-oriented councilmen and two-party systems on the one hand, and job-oriented councilmen and one-party systems on the other. This seems a very convincing explanation, although from my research it appears that it might be useful to break the 'job-oriented' category down into two: one aspect is the enjoyment of prestige and status elements, including attendance at functions and membership of committees such as the town-twinning committee,[36] and the other is the desire to be

[35] J. Fenton, *People and Parties in Politics* (Glenview, Ill. Scott, Foresman, 1966).

[36] 'Town-twinning' committees may be unfamiliar to non-British readers. Local authorities often arrange links with towns or areas in Europe to facilitate exchange visits and develop friendly relations. Sometimes committees are established to deal with these exchanges and members on the committee can have preference when entertainment or visits are arranged.

of service to the community generally (without holding a particular view of specific services). Councils made up of, or led by, issue-oriented individuals will be much more likely to be committed to the expansion of services than those councils where councillors are mainly concerned with their civic position. Officers who are also committed to service development or are in a position of wishing to further their career and standing within the profession will also be likely to be attracted to councils with an issue orientation, thus resulting in consensus at levels of service provision much higher than that achieved by many job-oriented councils.

Again, one can speculate on the reasons for the connection between party systems and actor orientations. Two-party systems require elections to be fought, and voter inducements have to be offered by both sides. Issues become prominent in these circumstances and could encourage individuals who are committed to issues to stand, partly because they are searched out and recruited on that basis, but also because they are likely to achieve higher positions on the council than would individuals who are not able to fit the prevailing norm, and high positions are an inducement to stand. On the other hand, in a one-party system the party in control can virtually guarantee to win and therefore has no incentive to raise policy issues. Recruits cannot be attracted by the issues but only be the advantages of the 'job': joining their friends in serving the community, or enjoying a civic position.

Although it seems plausible that issue orientation and two-party systems are related, if one looks at the areas or authorities which have a two-party system one sees that there are at least two variants. Two-party systems sometimes occur in areas which appear relatively homogeneous in terms of social conditions, where the population may hold similar attitudes and have somewhat flexible party allegiance, thus having to be wooed for their votes on the basis of issues as suggested above.[37] However, there are also two-party areas

[37]   See R. T. McKenzie and A. Silver, *Angels in Marble: Working Class Conservatives in Urban England* (London: Heinemann, 1968) for a discussion of 'secularism' as an ideological basis of working-class Conservatism.

which are made up of two or more communities which are sharply divided in terms of social class, social conditions and party commitment. In these circumstances it may be differential turnout alone, affected by such things as views on the central government's position, or party organisation, which decides who shall control the council. Issues here may be irrelevant. It may therefore be the case that while issue orientations may be found in two-party systems, it may not always be that two-party systems result in emphasis on service issues.

It is at this point that we can see a relationship between some of the concerns of this essay and the interests of some of the other contributors. The socio-spatial patterning of communities within a local authority affects the kind of party system which is created, whether it is one-party or two, and whether there is an issue orientation or not. There may also be a correlation between the socio-spatial structure and the attitudes discussed in the previous section. Future researchers will therefore need to look more closely at the relationship between socio-spatial dimensions and variations in service provisions as well as at the mechanisms by which this relationship is mediated.

Causal Processes and Techniques in the Modelling of Policy Outcomes

Bleddyn Davies

The statistical modelling of the causes of variations in policy outputs is still at an early and unsophisticated stage of development. Although it has already yielded much in the area — as much as older techniques of analysis — its future contribution will be far greater. But this will not happen until there exists a larger body of really careful, intelligent and scholarly research literature which is universally understood by a substantial number of research workers who have mastered the techniques of model-building with sufficient thoroughness to incorporate complex causal processes with precision. If this were a new area of physics, we should not have to wait long. But for bad reasons as well as good we are prejudiced against complex methodologies, and energetically promote new areas and methods before we have begun to reap a harvest from work based on the last set of new ideas. We may therefore have to wait. But there is no doubt that the preconditions will one day exist.

When the great day dawns, we shall need a paradigm. That the preconditions do not as yet exist at least has the advantage that no one need yet set themselves the daunting (and pretentious) task of putting together the main features of the paradigm. Indeed, to attempt to do so now would probably be futile: if an impressive and even in some sense a 'valid' attempt, it would not be acceptable enough to survive. With relief, we can retreat to the easier but more useful job of making one or two hopefully sensible suggestions about the development of theory and their operationalisation in models — suggestions about features of the real world that the would-be paradigm-creator would have to take into account.

Fig. 1 is intended to help structure the subsequent discussion. Firstly, it asserts that factors operate at varying levels of causal priority, the subject of the first section. Secondly, it incorporates the importance of values. Some difficulties of handling 'values' are discussed in the second section. Thirdly, it includes the mysterious terms 'need', 'supply' and 'demand', some aspects of whose interrelationship are discussed in the third section. Fourthly, it includes some factors that affect the cost and production functions of service providers.

CAUSAL PRIORITY

One of the most acceptable features of Fig. 1 is its assertion that causal factors are of differing degrees of causal priority. In the diagram they are grouped in four classes of increasing causal priority. Some environmental factors are exogenous — or as nearly exogenous as makes little difference so far as many outcomes are concerned. Although some policy outputs can influence the basic economic and therefore occupational structure of an area, they do so only to a small degree for the period of time over which the nature and relative strengths of processes remain sufficiently similar to describe in a statistical model. Such exogenous factors influence outputs and outcomes both directly and indirectly (via their effects on variables of intermediate causal priority). The characteristics of an area that make it more costly to produce outcomes of a standard quality may influence the expenditure levels directly, but these factors (such as sparsely distributed populations) also strongly influence salient features of local politics and other intermediate causes, and so affect outcomes indirectly as well. It is surprising that few of the studies have yet attempted to measure indirect as well as direct impacts by constructing simultaneous equation models. In literature which uses such models there has been little discussion of identification problems and particularly of the assumptions about the causal processes implicit in the different ways of securing identification. These assumptions are often important features of the model. One doubts whether those who have received their research training within the last decade will tolerate the absence of such

VIRTUALLY EXOGENOUS	CAUSALLY INTERMEDIATE	THE DECISION-DETERMINED FEATURES OF THE ORGANISATION	OUTPUTS AND OUTCOMES
Need-generating characteristics and n_i*	Consumer demand n'_i and v''_i†	Scale in the range of need-meeting activities	Supply: levels and patterns of outputs and (given the pattern of demand) outcomes
Other social characteristics of populations	Pressure group activity		
Cost-raising factors	Local electoral balance of national parties	Centralisation/decentralisation of decision making	
The local tax base			
Broad community values	Values of influential elites	Professional power and diversity of values	
Policy of superior governments	Resaux	Values of leading politicians and executives	

* See equation (1) p. 92
† See equation (3) p. 95

Fig. 1   The causal priority of some determinants of the supply schedule of outputs and outcomes in the personal social services

discussion much longer. One hopes that they will not.

Although the general proposition that some causes operate indirectly as well as directly through intervening causes is generally accepted, even some very recent research is conducted as if this were not so. Firstly, there are case studies using both the decisional and the reputational method which do not make even a token obeisance to the indirect influence of exogenous variables. But frequently these are studies which are almost self-consciously a-theoretical: they set out merely to tell a story, and are not interested in using and developing theory — indeed they make little use of literature of any kind. The authors cannot be called political scientists; they have implicitly turned their backs on political science and would presumably eschew such a title. Although the material they produce is frequently of value to the political scientist, they do not attempt to generalise — to create or develop the general hypotheses upon which depends the power of science.

Secondly, there are the studies whose focus is microscopic, but which are explicitly theoretical, although they do not relate the small system they are studying to the broader system of which it is a part. Since any model is a subsystem of some more general system, no one would doubt that this is a legitimate strategy in certain circumstances. For instance, it is legitimate if the writer defines his system in such a way as to include all the main causal variables, or omits only variables that do not statistically interact with the factors he takes into account and are uncorrelated with the factors studied. It can be legitimate also if the context has some of the characteristics of a block-recursive system — a system in which there may be feedback or reciprocal causation within blocks but in which the relationships between the blocks are recursive, and in which the influence of the variables in the block on other factors in the model can be reasonably summarised as the influence of the block as a whole rather than of its individual component variables. An example of this second kind of study is the treatment of the relationship between political variables and some social characteristics of communities in models whose focus is the explanation of the systemic operation of administratively uncoordinated services.[1] The relationship between political variables and some community characteristics may form a block of reciprocal, non-recursive relations which is recursively related to service outcomes. In order to understand the impact of the political variables on the system of services, it is not necessary to disentangle the reciprocal relations within the block.

A third type of study underestimates the impact of exogenous factors (though it may not completely deny them) because it uses a methodology whose bias leads to the understatement of the influence of exogenous factors. As the American evidence accumulated, it became clear that research workers investigating similar contexts with different techniques emerged with much the same listing of important causal factors. If one is therefore content with a body of theory that does not explain the relative importance of causal factors in different contexts, which technique the researcher uses may be less important than other qualities of the work (and the worker). However, it is clear that we are no longer content with non-quantitative understanding. The focus of discussion is now the degree of importance of exogenous factors compared with endogenous factors, and individual factors of each type compared with one another. One may quote a British example of a general issue that seems to have been settled for the United States some time ago. Is it generally the case that it is what the actors in the political process perceive to be important that are the crucial influences on outcomes, and that these 'imports' are not greatly affected

[1]   In the 1960s many of the personal social services in England were not administratively co-ordinated with one another, or with other services (like some health services) which contributed to meeting the same social care needs of the same types of people. Yet it was clear from comparisons of service provisions in different areas that the role of each of the services was interdependent with those of others in the same need-meeting system. Much evidence exists about the processes which allow this systemic interdependence. However, the actors in the processes were to a high degree unconscious of the systemic interdependence of services' roles. See Bleddyn Davies *et al.*, *Variations in Services for the Aged* (London: Bell, 1971); *Variations in Children's Services among British Urban Authorities* (London: Bell, 1972); *Planning Resources for Personal Social Services*, James Seth Memorial Lecture for 1971 (London: Bookstall, 1972).

by pressures generated by the external environment? Such seems to be the position taken by Dearlove as a result of his study of the Royal Borough of Kensington and Chelsea.[2] Or, as the author of a study of Wolverhampton concluded, is it more generally the case that 'the environment posed the problems and influenced the way the councillors looked at them and the solutions that emerged . . . [but] above all, the decisive factors shaping the political process [and so presumably the structure of outputs] were the elected members and officials'.[3] Or do largely exogenous environmental factors have a dominating and pervasive effect on the issues, the demands made on the system, and on who the actors are? It is difficult to argue that case studies can provide a complete answer, even when the results of many are available and comparable, and relate to areas that are archetypical of well-populated types of local authority.

This is not to imply that the case study approach does not have a valuable role to play. No one would argue that an understanding of the 'grammars of meaning' used by councillors to structure their world does not contribute greatly to our understanding of policy formation, merely that such understanding does not necessarily reflect the true causal importance for policy of the environmental factors external to the authority. The techniques associated with the case study approach almost inevitably produce a biased picture of the relative importance of causal factors, the biases conforming to those present in the grammars of meaning of the participants. Statistical model-building can incorporate biases of its own. The techniques explain as much as possible using the variables (usually heavily weighted with environmental

---

[2]   J. B. Dearlove, *The Politics of Policy in Local Government* (Cambridge: Cambridge Univ. Press, 1973). Dearlove attacks the application of statistical model-building techniques to the explanation of policy of outputs with more vigour than precision. His opinion seems to be based on a small number of American reviews and studies published in the 1960s rather than on the better and more recent literature — even the better and more recent British literature.

[3]   G. W. Jones, *Borough Politics* (London: Allen & Unwin, 1966).

variables), and so can overstate the importance of the factors. Whether or not they do so depends mainly on the degree to which the researchers subject themselves to the testing and development of a precise causal argument compatible with a wide and well-organised range of other (often non-quantitative) evidence rather than merely dredge for likely relationships. There are no reasons for claiming that any one technique is superior to others.

VALUES AND THE VALUATION OF ARGUMENTS IN THE OBJECTIVE FUNCTIONS

One would seek in vain for precise agreement about the dimensionality of values between studies, though some dimensions (like the public-regardingness of Banfield and Wilson[4] or the nine dimensions distinguished in Jacob *et al.*[5]) may well have pervasive causal importance. But even such pervasive value elements may be operationalised most effectively in different ways depending on the output or outcome being explained. Since there is a sense in which the operationalised medium is the theoretical message, it is therefore inevitable that even the most general value concepts used to explain different outcomes will be slightly different from one another, just as at a higher level of generality a political concept of Seeman's 'powerlessness' dimension of alienation would differ from an occupational concept of the same dimension.[6] Thus the value dimensions most useful in the explanation of (say) variations in policy outputs in the police services might differ from those most useful for explaining variations in social welfare for the aged, not only because the two sets of outcomes would be affected by some values which are of little interest to outputs other than the ones being studied, but also because the more pervasive values might be best operationalised in slightly different ways in the two contexts. The test of a conceptual apparatus of theory

4　J. Q. Wilson and E. Banfield, 'Public Regardingness as a Value Premise in Voting Behaviour', *American Political Science Review*, Dec 1964, pp. 816-87.

5　International Studies of Values in Politics, *Values and the Active Community* (New York: Free Press, 1971).

6　M. Seeman, 'On the Meaning of Alienation', *American Sociological Review*, Dec 1959, pp. 783-91.

and the methods of operationalising the concepts it uses is the prediction and invention it allows. In the grey world of fictions of limited truth that constitutes scientific theory, it would be surprising if precisely the same concepts identically operationalised best passed the tests for all outcomes. There are, of course, additional practical reasons why procedures should not always be identical: for instance, the indicators of the general concepts may well be based on measurement instruments that have to be adapted to (for instance) national circumstances. However, the present lack of agreement about the pervasively important dimensions of value differences appears to be greater than is necessary. One would expect a more standardised approach based on increased agreement about what is pervasively important to emerge in the near future as evidence accumulates. An advantage of having a number of general concepts of pervasive influence would be that it would then be feasible to devote more adequate resources for developing batteries of questions.

As in many other areas of social science, the methods of operationalising concepts have been crude. Indicators with large error variances tend to attenuate apparent correlations — to make the mean scores on value indicators in different categories more similar. Are the differences between the Scandinavian countries really as small as is suggested by Allardt's important and professionally executed work?[7] Or are the error terms in the indicators large enough to make substantial national variations seem so?

Less obvious than the need for some agreement on leading dimensions of value is the need clearly to distinguish *values* (which influence the arguments in the objective function, the function that it is the objective of the individual or group to maximise) from *valuations* (the weights that are attached to each of the arguments in the objective function itself). The problem of inferring the weight of objective functions in a political context has had insufficient attention from political scientists, although the problems have been faced squarely in

[7] E. Allardt, *About Dimensions of Welfare*, Research Report 1 (Research Group for Comparative Sociology, Univ. of Helsinki, 1973).

other contexts. The central problem is that even where (if ever) values enter directly into decision-making because they are arguments of the objective functions of actors, valuations are conditional upon expectations about outcomes, expectations about costs, and various constraints. The perceptions of all these vary between actors, and for any output there can be a large number of specific considerations subsumed under each of four broad categories: values, expected outcomes, expected costs, and constraints. The evaluations of all sets of factors have to be made simultaneously if they form part of a decision. The combination of expected outcomes to be aimed at is dependent upon the resources to be allocated, and the valuation weights attached, to each outcome at that level of resources, which in turn is dependent upon the relationship of benefits to costs through time of alternative expected patterns of outcome, where the costs depend partly on the patterns and quantities of outputs (which are subject to various constraints). If these were set out in an equation form, the result would be a set of non-recursive simultaneous equations each with a large number of terms. Of course in most (perhaps all) circumstances values themselves are not arguments in the objective function, although they influence these arguments. Where the influence of values on valuations is indirect, this argument is doubly strong.

It follows that for two reasons it is illegitimate merely to regress outcomes on values in order to estimate the valuation weights. The first is that the other variables which affect outcomes are in no way taken into account. To know what to control is itself a formidable task, since it requires a good understanding of the implicit and explicit factors which affect choice. Simply to ignore the other factors influencing an output would seem to be extremely dangerous. The second is no less important because it is technical. It is that even where values themselves are among the arguments of the objective function, this equation is embedded in a *system* of relationships; for this reason, the error terms of the equation in the system are not uncorrelated, and the direct application of least squares to our equation will not yield unbiased estimates of the parameters, even if sample sizes are unbiased. The least squares estimates of the impact of values on outcomes will be biased upwards if the implicit structural equations of our model are correct. The need to recognise that the derivation of valuation weights is embedded in implicit decisions which depend on other variables whose weights are simultaneously determined with the valuation weights exists irrespective of the range of other variables controlled for in the regression equation. Except under most unlikely assumptions, the single equation which is intended to be the model's structural equation can be used to estimate valuation weights.

How practical is it therefore to establish the impact of values on outcomes? This depends partly upon the complexity of the objective function of each actor in the decision process and of other actors who influence decisions, and partly upon the diversity of actors involved. The latter depends greatly on the degree of centralisation of the decision-making process for the range of outputs considered. There are some ranges of outputs which are sufficiently of public concern for the values of the general public to have a strong impact. Mancur Olsen has provided the analytic tools which could be operationalised to indicate where this is so. It is not difficult to provide examples; one circumstance about which there is a large literature concerns the conditions in which there might be an active micro-politics of the issues relating to the decisions. Such contexts are made more difficult to handle because it is precisely in such circumstances that public opinion is most responsive to established or emergent political leadership, and in which shifts in values are most likely to occur. In other words, in those circumstances in which the values of the public at large are most likely to have an influence, the lower-order values whose effects are most specific to the outcomes being investigated can be least reasonably regarded as exogenous. Many fields are unlikely to be of such interest for most members of the public for there to be a powerful reciprocal causation between public opinion and decision-makers. Glastonbury *et al.* have shown, for instance, how strongly the public perceptions of the British social work services in the 1960s reflect pre-rather than post-war ideologies.[8] In this case the public

---

[8]   B. Glastonbury *et al*, 'Community Perceptions and the Personal Social Services', *Policy and Politics*, Mar 1973, pp. 191-212.

perceptions probably act more as occasional constraints than
as sources of continuous influence. The apparent influence of
the number of linkages joining strong power groups to one
another and to a co-ordinating agency (featured by Aiken
and Alford[9] and by Turk[10]) reflects the public concern with
the issues as well as such factors as the degree of horizontal
differentiation in the social system.

The degree of centralisation of decision-making (and therefore the complexity of the process of the statistical models
needed to estimate the influence of values) depends greatly
on the number and power of the professional groups concerned. One would hypothesise that the larger the number of
professional groups concerned, the more dispersed they are
throughout the organisation, and the greater their power, the
more decentralised is influence likely to be within the
organisation whose outputs and outcomes are being studied,
and the more likely it is that the professional ideologies
developed nationally will influence local outcomes through
linkages between professionals. Here again, organisation
theory (rather than the theory of public goods) suggests what
policy outputs might be most influenced in this way, as has
been shown   for England and Wales by Greenwood and
Hinings.[11]

The British personal social services (social care services for
families) provide a good example. There is a diversity of
sources of value judgements, reflecting the mix of bureaucratic, commonweal and service characteristics of social welfare organisations. The several groups of professionals involved may legitimately have an influence because of their
expertise, their understanding of client problems because of
the immediacy of their contact with them, and their normative commitment to the good of the client. The politicians
may do so because they are elected or selected in order to

9   Michael Aiken and Robert Alford, 'Comparative Urban Research
      and Community Decision-making', *New Atlantis*, Winter 1970, pp.
      85-110.
10   H. Turk, 'Interorganisational Networks in Urban Research',
      American Sociological Review, Feb 1970, pp. 1-19.
11   R. Greenwood and C. R. Hinings, 'Local Government Organisa-
      tion', *Policy and Politics*, Mar 1973, pp. 213-21.

face the issues of the resource and welfare consequences of alternative sets of priorities on behalf of the community. Administrators of various kinds may do so because their special knowledge, experience and position in communications networks give many of them a better basis for judging the practicality and some of the consequences of actions. There is widespread agreement with the proposition that clients and others closely affected should have a formal right of participation also. Three, if not four, of these groups influence policy outcomes (and in doing so constrain the influence of any one group). All four have identifiably different imports and value systems and there are sub-groups within the main groups with different systems. But as is generally so, in all four cases the value systems affect policy outcomes through decisions in which the value contribution is not usually clearly and separately distringuished. Most of these are decisions about the relative needs — that is, about priorities in the allocation of resources. Typically, the decisions allocate the resources of a single service or combination of services between clients or client groups, or allocate finance to inputs correspondingly identified with services for broad client groups.

It is in such circumstances as this that the political analysis of the effects of values on outcomes can be most interesting and the importance of estimating valuations properly most important. The estimates of valuations would reveal the degree of consensus or dissensus within the organisation, and between actors in the organisation and recipients and potential recipients. Not the least of the merits of estimating valuations is the basis it provides for the mapping of patterns of consensus within organisations. If such patterns are statistically demonstrable and correspond with groupings within the organisation — in social service departments, for instance, professionals and administrators, qualified field workers compared with unqualified workers, more compared with less recently trained, community workers compared with case workers, unpaid voluntary workers compared with salaried employees, field workers compared with residential workers, cosmopolitans compared with locals, recipients compared with workers — the analysis of patterns of variation can provide the basis for statistical models testing conflict theories of the determination of outputs. In this way one can explore the internal inconsistencies of the organisational contexts, and thus the way in which values and ideologies influence (and are influenced by) the way in which actors create conflicts and resolve them through time, and so affect the structures of outputs. In this context a dialectical paradigm may contribute more than a functional approach.[12]

Is the estimation of valuation weights and the assessment of the impact of values on them so complex as to be unresearchable in this decentralised situation? In principle, it should not be. The conflict centres on the valuations themselves and the definition of the dimensions which define the groups of comparable persons in need. Underlying the patterns of valuations are judgements reflecting different causal theory and therefore the expected consequences of interventions as well as judgements about the relative diswelfare about states, and differences of values. Some of the same factors also underlie differences in the definition of the relatively 'homogeneous' groups to be compared. Finer classification would produce groups of client states which could be aggregated in such a way as to make the same data base appropriate for estimations for the various groups; and a more elaborate statement of objections could likewise contain the objectives important to all groups. The price of such conflict-oriented studies would be twofold. Firstly, in any one study the coverage of output groups and therefore the generality of the conclusions would have to be reduced. Secondly, index number problems would arise. For instance, using the mean valuations of valuer group I, client type A might have a lower per capita valuation than client type B; while using the mean valuations of valuer group II, client type B might have the lower valuation. The degree to which such index number problems can be shown to arise from a set of valuations — the degree to which the acceptance of some weights or case classification rather than others leads to

[12] See J. K. Benson, 'The Analysis of Bureaucratic — Professional Conflict: Functional versus Dialectical Approaches', *Sociological Quarterly*, Summer 1973, pp. 376-94.

different positions — is itself an indication of the potential power of a conflict theory in this context. The comparison of alternatives using what amount to index numbers is all the more fruitful in the decentralised organisation because of the large number of groups whose valuations may differ systematically. The technical problems of estimating the valuation weights are not such as to make it impossible to estimate them even in the more complex decentralised situation.

I therefore think that the valuation weights are estimable as long as the logic of choice that actors use (or would use if they could) is reasonably understood, and as long as the factors involved in this logic of choice are comprehensible. The problem is of four kinds: the assessment of values and valuation weights for each actor or group of actors taken in aggregate; the assessment of the values and valuation weights of non-actors like potential recipients; the assessment of the relative influences of the actors on the output; and the assessment of the influence of non-actors. The first of these can be tackled either by analysing actual behaviour or by causing actors to simulate the decision-making in which valuation weights are embodied. For this to be successful, it is essential that the actors should be required to apply the same thought-processes — the same logic of choice — as they would in their actual decision-making. In some contexts this limits the exercise to allocating specific resources to specific types of recipient where other circumstances which influence decisions are known. In some circumstances this involves individual decisions; in others, the simulation of group decision-making.

By varying hypothetical circumstances it is in principle possible to provide data which would make it possible to disentangle the valuation weights from the expectancies about costs, outcomes and other factors. The valuation weights for the objective functions of those (like potential recipients of services) can be estimated in basically the same way. This is already done by the cost — benefit analysis, although they do not in general handle the subjective evaluations of risk, and tend to assume that each component in the outcome can be traded off against money at a constant rate, unlike the methods used to fit multi-dimensional utility functions developed in operations research out of the work of Ramsey[13] and von Neumann and Morgenstern.[14]

The assessment of the impact of actors can be estimated by comparing the decisions that would be made in the absence of the constraint imposed by other given expected outcomes and costs, with the decisions that they would make in the presence of these constraints. The assessment of the impact of non-actors' valuations can similarly be directly estimable from a valuation exercise because they must form part of the objective functions of actors if they are to have a direct influence, except in so far as the influence operates via demand in the sense in which it is defined below.

NEEDS, SUPPLY AND DEMAND

It is frequently argued by writers on social policy that the concept of 'need' is so imprecise that the term should not be used. This reflects the absence of an adequate taxonomy of need concepts more than the absence of precision in the use of need concepts by individual research workers. In the absence of adequate taxonomies and elementary explanation it is not surprising that practitioners of social sciences which have not felt it necessary to define and operationalise concepts of need have underestimated the amount of work that has been done in other subjects.

It is beyond the scope of this essay to describe alternative need concepts, but it is necessary to define the concept used here; the quantitative dimensions of the three concepts (needs, supply and demand) will be seen to have closely similar definitions. By need in this context I mean

$$\sum_i (n_i v_i) \tag{1}$$

where n_i is the number of recipients (or potential recipients) of a service in problem state i, and v_i is the financial value of the resources that is judged to be appropriate to allocate to

[13]   F. P. Ramsey, *The Foundations of Mathematics and Other Logical Essays* (New York: Harcourt, Brace, 1931).

[14]   J. von Neumann and O. Morgenstern, *The Theory of Games and Economic Behaviour* (Princeton, N.Y.: Princeton Univ. Press, 1967).

alleviate the diswelfare of each person in the state, given the total amount of resources available and the relative prices of substitutable services. It is the sum of the products of the number of persons in each problem state and (in effect) the social valuation attached to intervention to ameliorate the state.

This is a definition of need whose operationalisation is most demanding on knowledge. Not only is it one which requires the estimate of the valuations of the objective function discussed in the previous section; but it is one that requires that this estimate be in pecuniary terms. Many of the concepts have been less demanding, measuring the needs in units of the physical resources required of a single service; or basing the implicit weights not on v_i derived by means of a valuation exercise of the type discussed in the last section, but on personal judgement or a crude estimate of what valuations are implicit in actual behaviour. Some have altogether ignored variations in the v_i between all but the broadest client states. For example, some have taken as the need measures for services for the elderly the number of persons aged 65 and over, thus ignoring the fact that a single male aged 80 and over had a probability of receiving institutional care a hundred times greater than a married woman aged between 65 and 69.[15]

By ignoring the variations in the v_i and the variations in the classification of client groups which different interested persons use, the social scientist loses the opportunity to use more powerful tools to study outputs and outcomes as the consequence of conflicting values. To the academic, particularly to the political scientist, indicators of the degree to which need evaluations differ, and the conflict consequences of these differences, are as important as indicators of needs that assume (or help to contrive) a consensus are to politicians of important subjects where this is so: the commitment of various groups of teachers to the competing aims of education, the way in which social workers interact with their context and other actors to create different need

---

[15] See Bleddyn Davies, *Social Needs and Resources in Local Services* (London: Michael Joseph, 1968) Table 22.

ideologies,[16] or the way in which different groups of workers
with different values and implicit bodies of causal theory
unwittingly cause the outcomes of activities to be compatible
with predictions made from their invalid theories.[17]

The estimation of n_i is more highly developed than is the
estimating of v_i, save that the client states distinguished tend
to be too general, and not to correspond to the groups to
whom the professional front-line allocators would wish to
attach priorities. For instance, a recent British study suggested that it was necessary to distinguish some sixteen client
groups in the allocation of social care services for the elderly.[18] It would not be possible to estimate the number of
persons in each of those twenty groups from the data for
small areas available in the British context.

The quantity supplied, operational in a manner compatible
with this definition of need, is defined thus:

$$S = \sum_j (v'_j q_j) \qquad (2)$$

where v'_j is the social valuation of output j, and q_j is the
number of units of it produced. The q_j can be defined entirely with the nature of the production processes in mind.
The supply concept is closely related to the need concept
because the v'_j of the supply concept amounts to a weighted
average of ratios derived from the v_i's discussed above. Although in principle the classification of output (and therefore
its valuation) could be made detailed enough to distinguish
important variations in quality, so that variations in quality
could be measured by the overall quantitative indicators, in
practice it is difficult to incorporate variations in the quality
of service in the measurement of quantities. Further, some of
the qualitative features of supply attach not to the unit of
service but to broader or narrower units, and are influenced
by broader factors. For instance, the degree to which recipients and potential recipients perceive applying for a

[16] G. Smith, 'Ideologies of Need and the Organisation of Social Work
      Departments', *British Journal of Social Work*, Spring 1972, pp.
[17] R. Minns, 'Homeless Families and some Organisational Deter-
      minants of Deviancy', *Policy and Politics*, Sep 1972, pp. 1-22.
[18] J. Brotherton *et al.*, *Manchester's Old People*, L.G.O.R.U. Report
      (Reading, 1972) pp. 44-5.

service as potentially stigmatising may reflect aspects of the way in which the individual service is provided; but it is also likely to reflect the manner of provision of all the other services associated with it in the mind of potential recipients. The measurement of quality for quantitative model-building is important for various reasons. For instance, many types of social service output — places in foster homes, places in residential homes, units of provision of domestic help, units of social work perhaps — are likely to decline in quality the greater is the rate of expansion and therefore, in some circumstances, the scale of provision. Therefore, in the discussion that follows, I shall distinguish between quantitative $(\sum_j (v'_j q_j))$ and qualitative variables. Again, alternative supply measures that use the valuations (v_i) of different groups would be important in the assessment of policy outcomes as the result of conflict.

The definition of the concept of demand used is:

$$D = \sum_i (n'_i v''_i) \tag{3}$$

The distinction between the n_i of eqn. (1) and the n'_i of eqn. (3) is that the n'_i are the subsets of n_i that actually bombard the agency with requests for assistance, or are referred there, or continue to receive the agency's assistance. The explanation of the shortfall between n_i and n is an important approach to explaining variations in outputs. The two components of demand have causes in common. For instance, both the $\sum n'_i$ — or, more directly, $\sum_i (n_i - n'_i)$ — and the v''_i reflect factors that make receiving the services potentially stigmatising. But the factors creating the stigma-potential of receiving services can differ in their relative importance as a deterrent to applying, and as a determinant of judgements about v''_i among those who applied; and in each case the degree of sensitivity to each dimension of stigma can vary greatly between client groups. Indeed, the stigma-potential of a service context is often of a catalytic nature: the context often provides an opportunity in which human interaction can reveal the potential for stigmatisation of attributes of an applicant or recipient that are unrelated to the official evidence of need.[19]

[19] Bleddyn Davies and Michael Reddin, *University Selectivity and Effectiveness*

Similarly, the level of unawareness of potential recipients about such aspects of the nature of services as their intended roles and eligibility criteria influence both $\sum_i (n_i - n'_i)$ and the v''_i.

That these causal influences among others reflect past supply conditions as well as other causes is well documented. The introduction of new services creates demands for them and thus alters both $\sum_i (n_i-n'_i)$ and the v''_i. Improvements in quality cause increases in demand mainly by reducing $\sum_i (n_i-n'_i)$. Differences in circumstances in which services are provided similarly control demand.[20] Quite subtle features of their provision have substantial effects on demand. Examples can be found in the study whose results have been referred to above. Consumers and potential consumers of means-tested free school meals from areas which were similar with respect to the proportion of children from poor families but with very different proportions of children receiving free meals revealed many ways in which authorities influenced the demand for free meals. In particular, there was an association between recipients and potential recipients' perceptions of the services as being potentially stigmatising, between their attitudes and the local authorities' efforts to publicise the services and respondents' knowledge of the services, between the regulations making it more or less easy to obtain services when eligible and the probability of consuming it.[21]

Similarly, past demand influences supply in a variety of ways. In the short run, the capital stock (physical and human) reflects a reaction to past needs and demands, and thus sets constraints on current production possibilities, affecting both v'_j and q_j of eqn. (2). Habits of mind in the perception of service problems sometimes tend to make current solutions more appropriate to past than to present problems. These again affect the v'_j. The allocation of current resources assumes that the demand will be related to that of previous years. If allocators were to assume bombardment

20   See Davies, *Social Needs and Resources in Local Services*, chap. 2. See also A. Harris, *Social Welfare of the Elderly* (London: Government Social Survey, 1968); and A. Hunt, *The Home Help Service in England and Wales* (London: Government Social Survey, 1970).
21   Davies and Reddin, *University, Selectivity, and Effectiveness*.

by Σn_i, not $\Sigma n'_i$, they would have to adopt a completely different set of v_i from those in practice assumed, at least in most circumstances, as was argued in *Planning Resources for Personal Social Services*.[22] Indeed, present demand influences supply to some degree. For instance, in a personal social service activity, providers and recipients implicitly negotiate a position about recipient needs. Where this negotiation is not mutually satisfactory either the recipient or the provider will often withdraw — as in social work.[23] Secondly, demand pressures can generate political activity by pressure groups or by recipients or potential recipients. Examples of such micro- and macro-political activity abound, and the effect is often powerful.

Therefore the demand and supply factors so operate in most conditions that the v'_i implicit in the v_j of the supply formula and the v''_i of the demand formula are equated and the values at which the equation occurs determine the v_i of the need formula. It is clear from their definitions that both demand and supply are positive functions of v''_i and v'_i respectively. Since v'_i and v''_i are measured in the same units (money), they can be indicated by the same axis of a diagram. Figs. 2(a) — (c) represent the two functions in a crudely linear form. (The client and service suffixes have been omitted.) The diagrams illustrate three contexts. In the first two, $dD/dV > dS/dV$, and in both the equilibrium values of v are dynamically stable: a disturbance would restore the equilibrium as long as the relationships between D and S and V_i remained the same, albeit by a process which may be indirect, depending on the lag structure of the model. The greater dD/dV, the smaller the change in V_i needed, and the smaller also the quantitative (and therefore resources) response needed to come to terms with a shift in the demand curve caused by a diminution of $\sum_i (n_i - n'_i)$. This conforms

---

[22] Davies, *Planning Resources for Personal Social Services*. The point was made in the context of a critique of utopian methods of estimating needs. The argument there was conducted in terms of need margins, but these are essentially the same as the v'_i defined here.

[23] For instance, J. Mayer and N. Timms, *The Client Speaks* (London: Routledge & Kegan Paul, 1973).

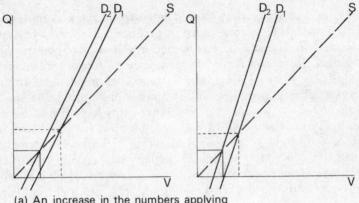

(a) An increase in the numbers applying

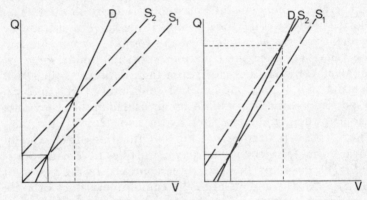

(b) A shift in the quantity supplied

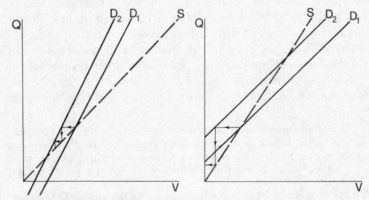

(c) Stable and unstable equilibria

Fig. 2

with common sense. The more a clientele accepts the values
of the agency, the less adjustment of values and quantity
supplied is required to meet the demands of an increased
number of such clients. Fig. 2(c) shows a situation where the
equilibrium is unstable. Where demand is relatively unre-
sponsive to past valuations system stability is clearly more
difficult to maintain. Again this is no surprise.

The simple diagrammatic models are in a number of ways
such a gross over-simplification as to be of little value as a
tool of analysis. In particular they ignore the shape of the
functions. The shape of the supply function would in general
be influenced by the v_j. In general, one would argue for both
cost and benefit reasons that both dV_A/dV_B and d^2V_A/dV^2_B.
(where V_A is the valuation of service A and V_B is the valuation
of service B and the V_i have the same meaning as in eqn. (1))
would be negative in any circumstances in which agencies
would operate. Secondly, the diagrams ignore conflicts
over values within the organisation. For instance, that this
has resulted in a low dS/dV in the past should not be taken
to suggest that it should do so in the future. The situation
might change quickly. The v''_i and so the v'_j of eqns. (2) and
(3) would vary according to the level of total provision.
Which dV_j/dR and dV_i/dR (where R is the total expenditure
on real resources) were high and positive in the relevant
regions would be of great importance. Thirdly, whether or
not the services formed part of systems of substitutes and
complements in the meeting of the general spectrum of needs
under study is vital. The interdependence of supply, demand and actors' perceptions of valuations takes place in,
and is greatly influenced by, the context of the need-meeting
system of services. The more substitutable at the margin are
the services, the more likely the system will be able to cope
with changes in demand at relatively low cost and with slight
changes in the valuations. (Fig. 2(b) is suggestive here.)

Such models as the one proposed have not been fitted.
Nevertheless, the general argument of systemic interdependence of supply and demand for services and actors' valuations
seems compatible with at least some of the statistical work.
There is clear evidence from models for the British social
services that where the capital stocks of services are unadjust-

able, variations in the rate of change in need cause systemic responses in the structure and nature of outputs. Since the personnel of services seem to be largely unconscious of this, and since in some cases there are no methods for co-ordinating the roles of the services that are components of the need-meeting system, the influence must work through variations in demand, not through the direct influence of differences in need on variations in the supply schedules. In the short run at least, it would seem that the stock of capital is not adjustable in response to demand, so that demand is deflected towards other components of the system, thus altering the roles of each service. For instance, county borough children's departments which had to cope with a heavy pressure of demand, but which did not have a compensating variation in the number of places in children's homes, tended to have a higher proportion of the children in foster homes — particularly foster homes outside the care authority's area; and of those boarded out outside the care authority's area, higher proportions tended to be supervised by the authority in that area rather than the authority whose legal responsibility it was. These authorities also tended to depend more on voluntary organisation homes. Also the courts tended to commit higher proportions of children to approved school than to children's department care. It is not simply that the children's service systems whose area's capital stock was under pressure relied more on facilities provided by other areas. The roles of the services differed in other ways. The rate of turnover of children in homes was higher. The authorities claimed that the effect of preventive work in keeping children out of care was greater. More children were in temporary accommodation in relation to the number in children's department care; and more were in health department nurseries and education department nursery schools in relation to the number in children's department nurseries. The children's service was affected in other ways. For instance, the authorities tended to appoint inexperienced and semi-qualified officers as a response to the high pressure of demand.[24] This is necessarily an over-simplification of complicated results; but the in-

[24]   Davies, *Variations in Children's Services.*

ference seems clear. The same was true of welfare departments. Although the supply of domiciliary services does not
appear to affect the number of places in residential homes,
the number of places appears to have an effect on the supply
of domiciliary services. Given the pressure of demand, therefore, the system finds a way of adjusting other services to
those which are in fixed supply in the short run.[25] Such
evidence that the services operate as systems, and that they
respond to differences in need-related characteristics (operating through variations in demand), is new, and is a discovery
of statistical model-building. Only three or four years ago,
Jean Packman's research had failed to discover it in one area
where it is now clearest, the inter-authority differences in
patterns of provision having been attributed to the policies
and preferences of decision-makers. The academic authority
on the personal social services who wrote that 'in the past,
the quality, extent and nature of the personal social services
have been largely supply-determined . . . the actual level and
pattern of need has played comparatively little part', reflected the state of understanding at that time. More recent
evidence from statistical model-building, and the theoretical
advances based on this evidence, show such statements to be
half-truths.

Although it is clear that the response to need-related
characteristics (through demand) is systemic, there are clear
signs that different dimensions of need call forth responses to
different degrees and of different kinds. Constraints on
supply help to cause this, but so may factors whose influences are more amenable to control. For example, capital
investment in residential homes for the elderly is more sensitive to the demographic structure than to bad housing,
poverty and their correlates, which have had a substantial
effect on decisions about the relative needs of individuals for
a place in a home. This may be partly due to the way the
central government controls loan sanctions. Some model-
building which takes into account that local authority allocations between broad departmental budget heads may be
intermediate in causal priority between the characteristics of

[25] Davies, *Variations in Services for the Aged.*

an area's population and its capital expenditure on homes, suggests that it is likely that the age structure of a population may have a stronger impact on expenditure on homes through its political impact on the broad strategic priorities of the council.[26] A second example of different dimensions of need calling forth responses of different kinds is that bad social conditions — poor housing, low incomes and related characteristics — tended to be associated with a reliance on approved schools rather than children's department care in the mid-1960s. There are several possible elements in an explanation of this: no doubt, the fact that higher proportions of children tended to enter care through the courts reflected differences between the courts' and children's department attitudes to treatment (although the courts' decisions are to some degree influenced by children's department policies), and the pressure on the scarcity of resources in children's departments, as well as the probability that delinquency is a more important symptom of child-care problems in the areas and elsewhere and that both the courts and the children's departments perceived that different treatment was appropriate.[27]

The causal processes involved in these relationships are complex. In particular, agencies that translate the unspecific feelings of potential recipients into demand for a service are important, because many recipients have little knowledge of service roles.[28] There are clearly circumstances in which supplies deliberately influence referral agencies' perceptions, so creating a supply — demand feedback. The causal processes underlying the relationships and feedbacks are extensively discussed in some of the model-building literature, though not in general in the British literature produced by political scientists. Of course, some need — demand influences are straightforward, as in a service in which a change in the environment (like a softening of the labour market) makes more eligible for service, and in which psychological and information barriers to consumption have been removed. The provision of free school meals may now be such a

[26]   Davies, *Social Needs and Resources in Local Services.*
[27]   Davies, *Variations in Children's Services.*
[28]   See Glastonbury, in *Policy and Politics,* Mar 1973.

service, though until recently the relationship between changes in need and demand has not been straightforward or strong.[29] However, the needs may not be those specified by the politicians. The school meals service was intended to help prevent malnutrition due to child poverty. Examination of the patterns of demand and the opinions of consumers show that by the late 1960s it had become an aid and subsidy to mothers' employment.[30] The political science literature should not neglect the effects of demand on v_i's in the context of need-meeting systems of services.

This emphasis on the importance of demand should not of course blind us to the direct impact of need-generating characteristics on supply. Although it is one most often postulated and purportedly described or tested in the literature, the indicators of need have in general been as unsophisticated as the models that contain them. A study of the arguments about social and economic policy suggests that it would be legitimate to postulate a concern for the correlation of outputs with area variations in need to a degree sufficient to postulate a normative principle of territorial justice as one criterion of the effectiveness of the system of central government supervision of local authority services – a principle operationalised in the test that outputs should be highly correlated with indicators of need-generating characteristics and should have the same degree of inequality as such indicators. However, statistical analysis has shown that the system has not been highly efficient in meeting this aim; and an analysis of the methods of control showed why this should have been so.[31] However, central government guidelines about levels of provision in relation to need have some influence, although they are not enforced, and although im-

[29] Bleddyn Davies, 'The Determinants of the Demand for School Meals', *Social and Economic Administration*, Mar 1971, pp.

[30] Davies and Reddin, *University Selectivity and Effectiveness*.

[31] See Davies, *Social Needs and Resources in Local Services*. The more extensive analysis of central – local relations conducted by Griffith also showed the crudity of the control mechanisms, though Griffith's evaluation was not conducted in the light of any clearly stated criterion. See J. A. G. Griffith, *Central Departments and Local Authorities* (London: Allen & Unwin, 1967).

portant dimensions of need are ignored by the guidelines.
Similarly, the control which the central government exercises
over the power to make capital expenditure is of influence.
Thirdly, a requirement that authorities undertake censuses or
surveys of need among a group (like the handicapped) increases demand for services, though there is evidence that
the surveys do not yield results that are comparable between authorities, and there is as yet no evidence that the
requirement has led to an increased correlation of needs and
provision. Fourthly, central government sometimes attempts
to exercise firm control on the mega-policies of a service.

Good examples are fixing the prices of school meals and the
eligibility criteria for free meals; publicising the income levels
at which people are eligible for free school meals; or influencing consumer perceptions and awareness by widely
advertising free school meals as an entitlement for which a
high proportion of children are eligible.[32] Fifthly, the corporate planning revolution has caused authorities to seek an
independent potential for research into needs. This will have
had little influence on outputs as yet. But although one must
accept that the direct impact of need on supply is of some
importance — and could with benefit be made much more
influential — one must conclude, particularly in contexts in
which services are complex in content, very divisible, and in
which their images with recipients and potential recipients
can be very variable, that this direct causal sequence does not
usually seem to be the main influence on outputs.

CONCLUSIONS

That we are still at the 'sealing-wax and string' stage in the
use of statistical modelling in political science is absolutely
clear from the three topics discussed in the preceding sections. These three are all important for a wide range of
model-building and are no less unsatisfactory in the way they
have been dealt with than other topics. One could equally
have discussed the integration of model-building into
multiple approach studies — the use of linkage models in the

[32]   Davies and Reddin, *University Selectivity and Effectiveness.*

analysis of *réseaux,* the implications of levels of measurement for the analysis of causal chains, or the handling of outputs in a manner that takes account of the nature of their technologies and 'quasi-technologies' (for example, the handling of joint supply, of technical progress, the concept of efficiency), the operationalisation of measures of various concepts of 'output', and other factors — and the implications of these for political analysis. One could also have discussed quite different aspects of the topics: for example, the data requirements for studying the characteristics of need-meeting systems. The three areas here discussed are in no sense those where the subject is best developed. Neither is it intended to argue that modelling will contribute nothing to progress in this branch of political science unless we use the most sophisticated techniques. The achievements of the 'sealing-wax and string' period have been remarkable. But the most important contributions will be made only when our techniques more nearly match the complexity of the problems we tackle.

Urban Politics as Political Ecology

Oliver P. Williams

Human ecology is concerned with the study of spatial distributions of social phenomena. Because urban settlements are examples of ecological patterns, urbanism, as an object of inquiry, may be viewed as a subset of human ecology. Ecological explanations of urban patterns, largely formulated by demographers, sociologists, geographers and economists, frequently stress such variables as migration, communality, resource locations and site advantages, but rarely political factors. Instead, politics is often treated as exogenous to the urban process, an element which interferes with its 'normal' functioning. While some political scientists have been concerned with space as a variable, their concern has been largely with global geopolitics, using simple territorial conceptions. This chapter will explore the benefits of using political variables as central, rather than peripheral, in the explanation of the urban spatial structure. It will also argue that political analysis in the urban context should be concerned with an interactional, rather than a territorial, notion of space.

No attempt will be made to review the very rich general literature on ecology and urban spatial research, as that has been amply covered elsewhere.[1] Nor will references to the political literature relevant to the analysis of urbanism be more than illustrative. Rather, an outline of the rationale and content of a field of inquiry, which might be properly styled urban political ecology, will be developed. To do this, it will be necessary to recapitulate briefly a language of urban political ecology which has also been stated elsewhere.[2]

[1] John Friedmann and Williams Alonso (eds.), *Regional Development and Planning* (Cambridge, Mass.: M.I.T. Press, 1964); Peter Haggett, *Locational Analysis in Human Geography* (New York: St. Martin's Press, 1965); and George A. Theodorson (ed.), *Studies in Human Ecology* (New York: Harper & Row, 1961).

[2] Oliver P. Williams, *Metropolitan Political Analysis* (New York: Free Press, 1971).

SPATIAL STRATEGIES OF SOCIAL ACCESS

All cities and settlements are, from one perspective, population convergences or clusters. Traditionally, the term 'urban' is not associated with just any population clustering, but only with those of a certain scale. However, scale is basically uninteresting in social and political analysis, unless it is an indicator of other more meaningful relationships. Urban sociologists have attempted to isolate the role transformations caused by increased scale and the associated characteristics of density and heterogeneity.[3] Other social observers have linked scale of settlement with a style of behaviour; hence the use of 'urbanity' as a synonym for sophistication in contrast to the rusticity of smaller settlements. Unfortunately, because of the large number of exceptions, the alleged behavioural patterns associated with scale of settlement break down. One can find many 'rustic' social patterns in large centres and, under conditions of modernity, the industrial farmer is often, in fact, very urbane. The role transformations which Wirth saw as part of the urbanisation process have not withstood the weight of evidence from subsequent empirical studies.[4] Because the scale-determined behavioural or way-of-life formulations of urbanism fail to hold up, an alternative is needed.

Assume that all settlements, that is, spatial agglomerations of population, result from purposive acts, and that this drawing together results in interactions that are inhibited by more scattered forms of existence. Spatial convergences reduce the cost of overcoming space as a barrier to interaction or, stated differently, population convergence results from widespread use of a spatial strategy for the purpose of selectively reducing the cost of social interaction. As our conception of urbanism needs to include unsuccessful as well as successful efforts of the spatial strategy, it is necessary to focus on a broader set of phenomena than interaction. For this reason,

[3] Louis Wirth, 'Urbanism as a Way of Life', *American Journal of Sociology*, July 1938, pp. 3-24.

[4] Scott Greer, *The Emerging City* (New York: Free Press, 1962) chap. 3; Janet Abu-Lughod, 'The City is Dead — Long Live the City: Some Thought on Urbanity', in Sylvia Fleis Fava (ed.), *Urbanism in World Perspective* (New York: Thomas Crowell, 1968), pp. 154-65.

we must introduce the term 'social access'. There is an enormous amount of energy spent in city building, which is designed to make interactions available or possible, but much that is intended by the actors never takes place. The incentives for city-forming social access acts are extremely varied. Historically, the major purposes have been primarily for mutual support (safety and military power), economic advantage (scale economics) and information gain (religious, commercial, cultural).

Let us examine the spatial-social access nexus to see if it yields a satisfactory conception of urbanism for use in political analysis. To recapitulate: urbanism is the use of location and space to structure social access. When man locates himself in relationship to others, or endeavours to locate others in relationship to himself, for the purpose of controlling or channelling social interactions, then he is engaging in the primordial urban act. However, if locational considerations are marginal or peripheral to the achievement of the major preoccupations or concerns of a social group, then spatial strategies will be subordinate in structuring social interaction. Under these circumstances, city formation may not occur. As location becomes increasingly important or advantageous in making the most salient interactions possible, the urban strategy is given priority. Urban-oriented behaviour is widespread in all societies, but only when many use a spatial means of structuring access to one another on a continuing basis does the urban settlement emerge. As the number of persons involved in locational strategies vis-á-vis one another increases, the social processes become more and more complex. It is this complexity of social relationships that has led scholars to view urbanism in behavioural transforming terms. However, in fact there is no necessary linear relationship between scale of settlement and complexity of social relationship. There have been large cities with essentially rigid, village-type social interaction patterns. However, increased complexity of social relationship normally accompanies increases in urban scale.

With increases in scale or complexity in locationally oriented social access strategies, a competitional element enters. There are competing claims for organising the spatial arrangement to suit differing sets of social priorities. This leads to the development of socially sanctioned ways for ordering and assigning locations, and with this step we enter the realm of urban politics. City building and rebuilding processes are inherently political because the way a city is constructed distributes differentially the cost of interaction among its members. The rules governing not only control of space, but also of movement, are political statements about the hierarchy of urban priorities. Who is allowed in, and the place assigned to them, are supreme examples of urban political power determination.

Because the treatment thus far may appear to be unduly abstract and remote from the concrete politics of a contemporary city, the language which has been introduced must be put to use. The whole purpose of this language is to bring together those things which are most related and to sep?_____ them from things less related. It is the assertion here th_____ spatial language can identify the set of related fact_____ policies which are general to all urban forms and car_____ out those factors and policies which may be mo_____ assigned to a different level of analysis, such a_____ individual behaviour, or other behavioural syst_____ step in explicating the content of the urban po._____ will be to argue the salience and importance of urba._____ in distributing important values.

VALUES FOR WHICH THE URBAN SYSTEM IS HIGHLY SALIENT

We usually associate the term 'urban policy' with such subjects as housing, public transportation, welfare services, police, water supply and parks. This list results from the fact that these services are often administered at the lowest governmental tier in many Western European and American nations.[5] There is, in fact, no such thing as a 'natural' local or urban service. Interestingly, at an international conference on metropolitan government held a few years ago, Polish

[5] Samuel Humes and Eileen Martin, *The Structure of Local Government: A Comparative Survey of 81 Countries* (The Hague: I.U.L.A., 1969).

scholars were assigned the task of writing on the functions of local government. Unconstrained by Western public — private distinctions, their article includes items such as warehousing and entertainment among the responsibilities of local loverment.[6] Thus, if we are seeking generality, it is preferable to identify urban policy with values distributed by urban systems, rather than with the functions of local governments. It is the thesis of this article that urban policies have important implications for the distribution of real income, opportunity, costs and satisfactions. These are closely related and overlapping terms and each will be dealt with successively.[7]

In this context, *real income* refers to purchasable goods and services, including public goods, for which some must pay, but not necessarily all, in order for the goods to be available for use. Life circumstances of various kinds affect the differing cost of items to various individuals. 'Getting it wholesale', living next to a berry patch, hitch-hiking or living at the end of a flat-fare bus line are little examples of the cash breaks of life circumstances. The issue here is how does an urban pattern systematically affect the distribution of goods and services? Is access distributed according to identifiable principles?

In market societies, locations are supposedly distributed through a pricing system. The price of land or rent reflects the bidding process. If the competition is among commercial enterprises, traditional economic theory states that the firm will occupy a site which can exploit it for the most profit.[8] Residential distribution reflects a similar bidding process, in which not only the affluence of the bidders, but their relative willingness to allocate portions of their budgets for housing, determines the outcome.[9] · From such a perspective, the

6   Julis Gorynski and Zygmunt Rybichi, 'The Functional Metropolis and Systems of Government', in Simon R. Miles (ed.), *Metropolitan Problems* (Agincourt, Ontario: Methuen, 1970).

7   Kevin R. Cox, *Conflict, Power and Politics in the City* (New York: McGraw-Hill, 1973).

8   R. M. Haig, *Major Economic Factors in Metropolitan Growth and Arrangement*

9   Richard F. Muth, *Cities and Housing* (Chicago: Univ. of Chicago Press, 1969) pp. 77 ff., 112-14.

urban pattern does not so much affect as reflect the distribution of real income. However, the actual distribution of urban space departs in many respects from this 'wheat pit' transaction model. In the first place, each location is unique. A place is the only point which has the same relationship to all other points. Urban places are not unique in this Euclidean spatial sense, as alternative locations can usually be found for carrying on most activities. But, in fact, satisfactory locations are always in limited supply, and the Euclidean analogy is appropriate since the value of a given location is affected by what goes on in all other locations. Thus, the value of a place fluctuates with the conditions of any buildings on it, what is changing around it, the access it provides to other places, and its symbolic meaning derived from past social transactions associated with it.[10]

A major way in which urban real income is affected, then, is through gains and losses in urban property values. If one is in a position to manipulate the forces that bring about the speculative gains, then income advantages are ensured. Those who can control strategic locations, which can be exploited for gain, continue to harvest income advantages over time. Commercial entrepreneurs who seek strategic access to customers are major participants in such efforts. Most national systems incorporate a variety of subsidies through tax laws and financing of real estate; thus, the rules for acquiring and holding urban locations provide a systematic bias to real income distribution.

Transportation systems are another source of urban real income distribution, as such systems powerfully affect the accessibility of locations. Every alteration in a network rearranges the social meaning of affected locations. Furthermore, the pricing and taxing system for construction and use of the transportation net further modifies the values of adjacent places. Cost — benefit relations for transportation are exceedingly complex, however, and one cannot assume the validity of simple cash transfers in making assessments.

The quality of municipal services generally, and the way in

[10]   David Harvey, *Social Justice and the city* (London: Edward Arnold, 1973) chap. 2.

which they are financed specifically, are also sources of real income differentials. If the quality of services varies by area, then those living in high-quality service areas receive a dividend, assuming a common means of financing services. It some cities the incidence of charges and distribution of services is either not related or inversely related.[11] Where local property taxes must defray local services, property-poor taxing districts may pay more for lower-quality services than citizens of richer districts pay for higher-quality services.[12] On the other hand, long-established high-quality local services may become capitalised into the price of property, thus providing for some recovery of tax 'investment'.

The distribution of *costs* connotes a mirror-image to income, but there is some advantage in using the notion differently. Here it will refer to unwanted consequences of urban events, rather than to taxations and fees, which may be conveniently included in the above treatment of real income. Costs may have monetary implications, but they are often difficult to assess. A clear example is adverse environmental factors: some live upwind and some downwind from the smelly places. It has been alleged that the class distinction between East and West London is derived from the prevailing direction of the winds. A new urban expressway not only brings access gains to some, but confers costs on others; those beside the road, who must breathe the exhaust fumes of the automobiles using the new access route, may be said to have borne a cost.[13] Whether governments can or should compensate for such damage is a question being debated in some nations.

Another example of differential cost distribution is furnished by the American experience with urban renewal in the 1950s and 1960s.[14] Urban renewal was ostensibly designed to

11 George Sternlieb, *The Tenement Landlord* (New Brunswick, N.J.: Rutgers Univ. Press, 1966) p. 231.
12 Oliver P. Williams, Harold Herman, Charles S. Liebman and Thomas R. Dye, *Suburban Differences and Metropolitan Policies* (Philadelphia: Univ. of Pennsylvania Press, 1965).
13 Anthony Downs, *Urban Problems and Prospects* (Chicago: Markham, 1970) chap. 8.
14 Herbert Gans, 'The Failure of Urban Renewal: A Critique and some Proposals', Commentary, Apr 1965, pp. 28-37.

make cities better places in which to live. The national legislation appropriately specified that renewal should begin in
those places legally defined as least fit areas for urban living.
Subsequent experience showed that definitions of unfit were
often culturally relative and that large area demolitions
inevitably destroyed the fabric of a living arrangement which
could not be easily compensated for in terms of alternative
housing or moving allowances.[15] Small businesses, which
were dependent on neighbourhood acquaintanceship patterns, had difficulty starting over. Older persons found it
hard to move and were less interested in the quality of
housing than in living among familiar circumstances. While
some of these costs can be translated into income or monetary terms, some obviously cannot.

It should be added that allowing neighbourhoods to
decline 'naturally' also involves costs, as the current aban-
doned housing problem in United States cities demonstrates.
Under conditions of population decline in an urban area,
vacant houses must increase, by definition, unless people
spread out to absorb each additional vacancy. Vacant housing
can have its own deleterious effects and can prove damaging
to neighbourhood life. Even demolition may prove to be
adverse, as the gaping holes produce a left-behind look.

Pollution, congestion, demolition, construction, growth
and decline all have their costs, as well as their income
effects. The political impact of these processes may be more
in public beliefs about possible consequences than in the
actual experience of them. One of the enduring examples is
the heterogeneous neighbourhood. When two or more groups
with highly divergent actual or reputed behaviour occupy a
close residential space, the potential for rancorous conflict is
high. Each group then claims a loss of public amenities, a
weakening of consensus, and therefore a decline in the weight
of its votes, adverse socialisation experiences for children,
lessening in public friendliness (perceived improprieties or
rudeness), or simply the end of public ease.

---

[15] Marc Fried and Peggy Gleicher, 'Some Sources of Residential Satisfaction in an Urban Slum', in Jewel Bellush and Murray Haus-
knecht (eds.), *Urban Renewal: People, Politics and Planning* (New
York: Doubleday, 1967).

Opportunities are occasions for individuals to better their position; opportunity is at the very heart of the urban idea. The urban settlement is, by its nature, a design to *increase* access to others as a means towards achieving goals. However, each urban system seems to work better for some than for others, as the opportunities are never uniformly distributed. Economic and social mobility is a complex process, and it is not the contention here that urban structure is the only agent of change. Yet it is apparent that the urban form does serve as a mediating structure, which can operate as either a handicap or an aid to social and economic mobility.

A major urban factor in social mobility, apparently, is the degree of social segregation of residential neighbourhoods. Ghettos, which might be defined as urban areas providing the social access least valued by society generally, are a good illustration. There is evidence that peer group experience is a major source for learning deviant behaviour. When peer learning is reinforced by the presence of adult models engaging in deviant behaviour and also enjoying social legitimacy in the ghetto subculture, then we have an environment which is conducive to preserving such behaviour from one generation to the next.[16] Some have also argued that the one-class neighbourhood has a self-limiting effect, in that social class is behaviour learned from early experience.[17]

If one-class areas are very large, one-class norms will tend to dominate the neighbourhood-based institutions. Schools are particularly vulnerable to class norms, and in the case of working-class areas this may adversely affect the possibility of class mobility.[18] To some extent, the comprehensive school proposals are based on this assumption, though the disapproved object is less one-class neighbourhood schools than functionally segregated ones. However, comprehensive schools in class-based boroughs may become class-based, not unlike the central city schools of some United States cities. Actually, the whole question of the relationship of education

[16]   D. W. G. Timms, *The Urban Mosaic* (Cambridge: Cambridge Univ. Press, 1971) chap. 1.

[17]   Herbert Gans, *The Urban Villagers* (New York: Free Press, 1962).

[18]   Peter Willmott, *The Evolution of a Community* (London: Routledge & Kegan Paul, 1963) pp. 115-17.

to social mobility is currently an object of major debate, as the causal relations are not well established.[19]

Closely related to the issue of ghettoisation and class or racial segregation is the treatment of newcomers. This is a major issue in rapidly urbanising nations and, to a lesser extent, in others. Generally, urban policies disciminate against the newcomer. New arrivals are motivated by the hope for improvement in their new places, and are engaged in a search for opportunity, in contrast to the certain and limited fate reserved for them in their places of origin. Cities have different policies regarding how newcomers are housed and what services, if any, they are entitled to.[20]

While the categories of income, costs and opportunities cover most of the values distributed and allocated through the urban system, they do not speak to the issue of how people perceive their circumstances, that is, their *satisfactions and dissatisfactions*. It cannot be assumed that everyone wants more of those things which are generally considered 'good'. There are a lot of trade-offs, and we cannot always predict what people prefer. For example, it was suggested above that older people often opt for the familiar in housing, even if it is inferior, in conventional terms, to unfamiliar relocation housing. Low-income families will often trade low taxes and no public services for high taxes and services. Thus, in comparing and appraising the performance of various cities, it is always desirable to remind ourselves that objective indices will not tell the whole story.

Because of the difficulty in identifying the indicators satisfaction is in fact a troublesome value to analyse. A satisfied populace may do nothing overtly political, so it is easier to talk of dissatisfaction. A variety of indicators have been used to measure urban dissatisfaction: riot, crime, graffiti, disfigurement of public places and traditional forms of political protest. Absence of these indicators may, however, be more a function of repression than a sign of satis-

[19] Christopher Jencks, *Inequality: A Reassessment of the Effect of Family and Schooling in America* (New York: Harper & Row, 1972).

[20] John Rex and Robert Moore, *Race, Community and Conflict* (London: Oxford Univ. Press, 1967).

faction. Certain Latin American dictators have been famed for their order and cleanliness fetishes and their cities are very well regulated and clean. Furthermore, it is often difficult to trace such adverse social indicators to their source, that is, to isolate the contribution of the urban arrangement to the dissatisfaction.

In summary, the foregoing argument has been that who — where relationships are of great significance; that the urban structure, which defines who shall be where and when, affects who has access to whom and influences whose mobility is best served, is a major source of value distribution; that these distributions can often be measured in very tangible terms, including real income and incidence of cost, as well as less easily measured values, such as opportunity and states of well-being.

THE LOCUS OF URBAN POLITICS

If the foregoing has demonstrated that who — where relationships are significant, it is now important to locate the decisions which affect the structure of these relationships. While some decisions are very obvious and receive great attention, others are obscured by their incremental nature. In the latter case we are concerned with the rules which guide the processes of urban development. While the creation of the rules may be perceived as political, they are rarely continuously reviewed and therefore are often accepted as givens. This is why urban processes are often treated as primarily economic or ecological, rather than political, in nature. The fact remains that we are dealing with a set of rules, collectively established, backed by sanctions, which have the effect of distributing values and maintaining order.

Before we turn to an inventory of rules which guide the incremental process, it must be stressed that urban processes are initially structured by decisions involving the locations of and relationship among major activity centres, the construction of major transportation and communication systems and the choice of technologies to be used in them. Indeed, one can define urban elites as those who dominate these decisions.

Historic turnovers in elite control have often profoundly altered cities as provisions are made to serve a new set of interests. The small, ancient Greek cities did not suit the access requirements of the conquering Hellenist military, so the small-scale, pedestrian-oriented building and street arrangements were replaced with new patterns, more suitable for wheeled military vehicles, pomp and display. The cramped, medieval cities were similarly reconstructed by the founding princes of the budding nation-states. The industrial barons of the coke-powered industrial revolution brought their sooty engines into the very heart of the city, subordinating the organisation of urban space to the dictates of steam-engine technology.

Modern city structures also reflect in major ways the values of ideology prevailing in dominant sectors. Certainly, for example, Soviet cities display the priorities assigned to housing and industry through the Stalinist period.[21] Automobile networks penetrating the core of cities show the important political place of the middle-class automobile owner in Western industrial cities. The new housing pattern in egalitarian Stockholm is a marked contrast to Madrid's.[22] At the same time, all modern industrial cities seem to have certain common characteristics, which reflect the constraints of a common technology and common requirements of production in an internationally competitive world. While the economic and technological realities may provide constraints for the political order, there remain large discretionary areas in which each urban polity carries out its who — where decisions.

The rules or 'contextual' policies which we are about to discuss are not listed in ignorance of the influence of non-political factors which affect cities. It is recognised that urban citizens are engaged in a constant process of adjusting their interaction patterns. Life cycles, job changes, demographic events of birth, marriage and death, household income allocation decisions — all can be used as explanatory

---

[21] Robert J. Osborn, 'How the Russians Plan their Cities', *Trans-Action*, Sep — Oct 1966, pp. 25-30.

[22] D. V. Donnison, *The Government of Housing* (Harmondsworth: Penguin Books, 1967).

factors. In addition, a city is both physical and social and, therefore, subject to decay. Neighbourhoods and their housing stock falter, commercial establishments become obsolete, fashions fluctuate, clubs and churches gain and lose members, and natural disasters occur. All of these social, ecological and natural events contribute to the building and rebuilding of the urban social access structure. However, the individual adaptations are monitored by a set of politically established rules, all of which are potentially selective in their application and impact. We now turn to these rules and policies which are a locus of urban politics.

Rules governing entry

One cannot enjoy the benefits of urban access unless one is on the urban scene. In most Western nations urban membership has no explicit barriers; however, some nations do control entry through occupational licensing or travel passes, as, for example, the Soviet Union and China.[23] The Soviet Union has made population movement a specific part of its urban policy in its effort to limit the size of Moscow[24] and build cities to the east.[25] In the case of limiting the growth of Moscow, rule enforcement proved a conspicuous failure, as too many industries and agencies arranged for exceptions in pursuing their particular organisation goals. China not only requires a permit for inter-city migration, but even for intra-city visitation in many cases.[26]

A more general set of entry policies pertains to making room for the newcomer. Except in the few cases where private industry supplies adequate housing to meet demand, some sort of queueing policy is essential. In most cases,

---

[23]   Ezra F. Vogel, 'Preserving Order in the Cities', in John Wilson Lewis (ed.), *The City in Communist China* (Stanford, Calif.: Stanford Univ. Press, 1971).

[24]   Roger Simon and Maurice Hookham, 'Moscow', in William A. Robson (ed.), *Great Cities of the World*, 2nd ed. (London: Allen & Unwin, 1957).

[25]   Peter Hall, *The World Cities* (London: Weidenfeld & Nicolson, 1966).

[26]   Vogel, in Lewis (ed.), *The City in Communist China.*

housing policies require newcomers not only to wait, but to wait longer than others.[27] Such customs are of particular political interest when they embody systematic ways of discrimination against classes of people.

Entry policies in many developing nations are largely expressed through decisions concerning squatter settlements. Once slums are crowded to the limit of human endurance, indigenous housing construction becomes an alternative.[28] Squatting, as the very term implies, involved illegal seizure of land for building purposes: it is obviously a particularly political act. To be successful, it requires sufficient political support on the part of the squatters to prevent the government from protecting the property rights of the landowners. Often, and particularly in the Latin American cases, squatting involves a set of political manoeuvres between the government and the squatters. Frequently the issue concerns not whether but where. For example, the policy may be to prohibit squatting close to the homes of the rich or in areas where industrial development is planned. Some Latin American squatting movements are extremely politically sophisticated and their complexity of organisation is great. During one night, lots are staked out, street systems delineated and community organisations set up.[29] Some major nocturnal land seizures have even been covered by television.

International immigration control is another form of entry policy. When the rural hinterland of a nation is no longer a major source of low-wage labour, an alternative may be sources from abroad. One issue in rule construction here is whether residence will be on a temporary work-permit basis or permanent immigration will be allowed. If immigration is permitted, is it to be under terms of full citizenship (in the urban sense)? Are immigrants discriminated against in housing? Is ghettoisation encouraged and are immigrants generally placed at the end of all queues?

[27] J. B. Cullingworth, *Housing and Local Government in England and Wales* (London: Allen & Unwin, 1966) chap. 5.

[28] William Mangin, 'Squatter Settlements', in Scientific American, *Cities: Their Origins, Growth and Human Impact*

[29] Ibid.

Rules and rights of land ownership

In English and American law, property ownership is a bundle of rights, each of which may be subjected to limitations in the public interest. The rights can be disassembled and limited and controlled one by one. Though one owns property, one may not be allowed to burn down one's house, build a pig-sty in the backyard or paint the premises with polka dots. The whole fabric of modern planning law stems from reasoning that declares there are wrong places for legitimate activities: the rendering works should be at the edge of town, preferably downwind. Planning limitations on development schemes are extensive, including specifications concerning use, quality of building, safety concerns, improvements, occupancy, physical bulk and location of structures on a lot, and a variety of easement strictures.

Public policy with regard to ownership rights varies widely throughout the world, and the variance in effective limitations supplies a principal source of divergence in urban development patterns.[30] Under English law, land as property slowly evolved into something approaching a commodity which can be bought and sold. The emergence of a land market made necessary legal clarity with regard to property titles. In Latin America, where the capitalist tradition was not so fully developed, ambiguity in land titles is the rule. This is now significant for urban development; with the title of vacant land frequently open to dispute, the legal basis for suppressing squatting is clouded.

Political analysis of urban ownership cannot be confined simply to the law, but must be extended to the discretionary application of the laws and to the behaviour of classes of owners. What owners are likely to do with their property is partly a function of their social position. Property held in trusts may be managed in a more conservative fashion than that held by speculative and expansive interests.[31] The scale of ownership may be another factor of interest. For example,

[30] R. W. G. Bryant, *Land: Private Property, Public Control*
[31] Oliver P. Williams and Charles R. Adrian, *Four Cities* (Philadelphia: Univ. of Pennsylvania Press, 1963) pp. 136-9.

the massive rental housing propeties held by major trusts and families in London prior to the Second World War were all similarly affected by post-war housing policies. When this massive quantity of housing was removed from the rental market as a result of rent control policy, the whole structure of housing in London underwent major changes.[32]

Tenure

In considering the matter of tenure, we are primarily concerned with residential property. Ownership, the more generally recognised basis of tenure, involves guarantees against eviction, except for purposes of eminent domain and non-payment of rates. In cities where home ownership is non-existent, rare, or declining as the major basis of residential allocation, alternative bases for tenure emerge. In some nations renters accrue tenure rights, a situation that usually coincides with some form of rent control. If owners are free to charge anything, tenure, of course, has no meaning. In Sweden there are not only tenure rights, but flats can be bequeathed, remaining in families for generations. Tenure rights may also be recognised for government-owned housing, a particularly important issue, as entry into public or government housing is usually based upon some standard of need. If need, particularly an income maximum, is enforced as a limitation on tenure in government housing, as it is in the United States, it means that all government housing will be populated by poor people.[33]

Development values

One of the more important public urban policies pertains to the matter of real property and speculative gain. Urban land has value (leaving aside the value of buildings) because of the access it affords to other places. Thus, development in one place helps to establish the value of other places within an accessible range. This results in the 'unearned increment' of

[32]   Oliver Marriott, *The Property Boom* (London: Hamish Hamilton, 1967).
[33]   John Macey, *Publicly Provided and Assisted Housing in the U.S.A.* Working Paper 209-1-4 (Washington, D.C.: Urban Institute, 1972).

land value, which Henry George wanted to expropriate for the public with a 'single tax'. It is also the profit the post-war British Labour government wished to eliminate for ever from the urban scene, with its Town and Country Planning Act of 1947. Speculative gain in urban areas under private property law is a major source of corruption and political manipulation. For example, if one can control the major policy decisions described above, then the impact of speculative gain can be directed. If one also has foreknowledge of location of major facilities, then speculation becomes a low-risk, but highly rewarding, proposition. Not surprisingly, such information often provides a source of graft, which is much more difficult for the public to ferret out than more obvious direct payoffs.

A permissive speculative policy is of significance in ways besides creating income for speculators. One possible effect is to encourage scattered development. Property in the path of urban development rises precipitously in value. Developers seeking lower per unit costs try to avoid these high land costs. By 'leapfrogging' to a more remote area they find a wider choice for development and lower prices. The result is scattered development, with implications for transportation and services costs to the future occupants.[34] If there are not controls to prevent it, an increasingly automobile-based urban form will produce this type of arrangement.

Rules for developers

Increasingly, cities are developed in fairly large increments. Development schemes, subdivisions or satellite communities are often designed to take advantage of scale economies. Large-scale developments afford opportunity for controlling more locational relationships and implementing plans which small developments cannot. With small increments it is much harder to integrate housing, commercial development, employment centres, parks and public facilities because they are not developed simultaneously.

In development schemes, both large and small, government

---

[34]   Marion Clawson, *Suburban Land Conversion in the United States* (Washington, D.C.: Resources for the Future, 1971).

or private, one issue is who assumes responsibility for what? Under private development there is often a bargaining process between the government and the developer over who takes care of the infrastructure. American suburban municipalities increasingly try to have the developers shoulder the responsibility for many capital improvements as a condition of gaining permission to build. Street, schools, parks, utilities and many amenities are often required as part of the subdivision plan. Such a strategy loads the costs of these facilities on to the purchase price of the new home, even when some of the new facilities will be used and shared by existing residences. This has been euphemistically referred to as upgrading the quality of residential stock. It means that only a higher-income population can buy in, thereby protecting the social status of those already there. Generally, developers try to assume as few of these extra costs as possible, because the lower the sale price of the completed houses, the broader the sales market.

An alternative to this bargaining process is to define in advance what facilities are public, and place their burden on the general urban public. Sometimes this gives the broader public one more weapon for controlling development, and it places limits on the suburban status game described above. A third alternative is to ignore the problem at the time of development. This usually means that there will be deficient or crowded facilities; the victims can only be predicted in particular circumstances.

Taxes and prices

Many of the foregoing rules on the rights and responsibilities of property ownership affect the costs of property at the point of development or sale. These costs are naturally a major factor in determining who may occupy what places. However, there are also a number of more direct pricing arrangements with implications for the allocation of access in urban systems. To illustrate, we shall consider local taxation, transportation and welfare.

A common source of revenue for supporting local government is the real property tax; the reason for this is that real property can be taxed but cannot be easily hidden from local officials or moved across a local government boundary to escape taxation. While the use of the property tax is easily explained in practical terms, its effects on the urban pattern are far from obvious.

Property tax liability is rarely directly proportioned to income.[35] The major hardship falls on older property owners with fixed incomes. Under conditions of inflation, the common fate of most industrial nations, the value of real property and property taxes rises faster than pensions; thus, property owners with fixed cash incomes are caught in the inflation squeeze. The property tax is also subject to evaluational difficulties, as 'true value' is difficult to establish for real property. This is particularly the case in industrial installations, large commercial properties and vacant parcels held for speculation. Where there are infrequent sales, it is difficult to establish value, thus contributing to inequities in taxation across functional categories of property.

Perhaps the biggest impact the property tax has on the urban structure in the United States is conditioned by local government boundaries in metropolitan areas. There is no necessary relationship between what a property yields in taxes and costs in services. Thus, it is theoretically possible to pay less and get more high-yield, low-cost land uses. The prizes are high-performance industries which take care of most of their own needs, but pay taxes. On the other hand, cheap houses filled with large families 'pay less than they yield'. This leads to a fiscally based land-use competition among suburbs around American cities in which there must be winners and losers. Among the London boroughs, despite the equalisation of rates, there remain enough differences in wealth levels so that it is also the case that fiscal considerations can affect land-use decisions.[36]

Depreciation write-offs, mortgage interest deductions on

35 Dick Netzer, *Economics of the Property Tax* (Washington, D.C.: Brookings Institution, 1966).
36 Thomas Anton and Oliver P. Williams, 'On Comparing Urban Political Systems: Residential Allocation in London and Stockholm', paper delivered at Annual Meeting of the American Political Science Association, Chicago, 1971.

income-tax obligations and other tax provisions are also powerful influences on property decisions. In many cases tax considerations can supply the marginal factor as to whether entrepreneurs build or do not build.

The impact of the transportation system pricing on urban form and pattern has been the subject of a great deal of analysis. A particularly favourite subject has been the influence of pricing on the use of mass transportation. However, the urban commuter seems to be a highly irrational animal who will go to great lengths and expense to travel from his place of work to the cottage of his dreams, if he can ever gain possession of it. Daily travel patterns become increasingly complex, as employment centres become more widely dispersed. The emerging transportation situation moves more and more urbanites in the direction of individual, self-propelled vehicles, causing greater and greater street congestion and a development pattern which generates the need for even more trips. Theoretically, if we could shorten the distance and reduce the number of everyone's daily trips, congestion would be reduced. One way to force people to move closer to work or to switch to public transportation is to make the urban use of the automobile extremely costly. Some would argue that if automobile users had to pay all the direct and indirect cost of automobile use, they would soon make different transport arrangements. At this point we can only say that the lowering of cost of automobile and motor ownership has brought about a revolution in urban form. What differential pricing systems might do towards altering cities is more in the planning that the political analysis stage, though the current fuel situation may turn these plans into realities soon. However, the effects of automobile lobbies on national transportation systems should not go unnoticed. The segregated highway fund in the United States has given tremendous power to highway-building sponsors and has only recently run into major opposition from urban residents suffering from environmental impact costs.

Finally, some attention needs to be given to the welfare implications of pricing and taxation in the urban system. As long as the city employs market criteria in its vast allocation system for the distribution of access, the poor, of course, will be continuously disadvantaged. A possible result is slums or ghettos, as those with the fewest resources occupy the least desired places. Slums have been the object of social revulsion for centuries, and during the past one there have been a variety of specific efforts to deal with them.

Many cities have areas which are officially prescribed as problems. The adverse indicators are high incidence of crime, ignorance, disease, blight and other forms of malaise. Getting people out of the slums becomes a public policy. If this takes the form of giving people more money, presumably those who are forced to live in slums simply for lack of income will move. However, income redistribution policies alone do not work, for there is no assurance, on the one hand, that the increased potential housing purchasing power will lead to an increase in housing supply, particularly an increase which will accommodate the former occupants of substandard areas. Because there is no assurance that substandard housing areas will disappear through abandonment, direct actions are usually pursued in the form of urban renewal, government-built housing projects, rent rebates or other direct action schemes. All these plans involve some form of government subsidy, as the idea that occupants of the substandard area will pay the improvement bill is impossible.

STATUS OF LOCAL GOVERNMENT

One of the general issues in urban government (discussed more fully in the next essay) has been termed the metropolitan government issue. Most major cities have been spreading out into their hinterlands. In this process, which has been going on for a century, but which was greatly accelerated by the internal combustion engine and the communication revolution, local government boundaries will crisscross the urban complex, unless they are constantly redrawn. Even in nations which frequently revise general local government boundaries, there is a time-lag. Thus, urban areas involve areal divisions of responsibility. Division of responsibility will occur not only across local governments, but also between levels of governments and special authorities.

Wherever there is decentralisation and separation, there is

the prospect of differentiation in policies. This may mean that residents of one part of an urban region h ʒ advantages over those in another, advantages which stem strictly from the jurisdictional arrangement. A further source of policy variance is the accessibility of the governments responsible for the urban decision points. This difference is not simply a matter of central ministry control over local· areas or local autonomy. Closeness to the people, or access to power, is not a function of distance to the relevant officer.

Political studies of governmental structures are much more frequent in the literature on local politics than the other points previously mentioned. All too infrequently, however, local governments have been studied with a specific concern for the implications of space and access. Urban actors are constantly looking for locational situations which improve desired access. A major issue is whether the determination of who gets ahead and who gets left behind is a function of the local governmental arrangement itself.[37] For example, a frequent situation in urban areas is the creation of autonomous local governments for elite residential areas. The fashionable suburb has been as recurrent a characteristic of industrial cities as were the foreign quarters of pre-industrial, colonial ones.[38]

URBAN SERVICES

Among the services usually administered at the local level are education, mass transit, police and fire protection services, environmental health, housing, urban renewal, libraries, traffic control. The idea of naturally local functions has long been dismissed; whether these services are in fact administered at the local level is a function of national policy. While there are no inherently local governmental functions, it is possible to isolate the urban component in any particular service area. A clarification of the relationship between urbanism and these functions can serve two purposes. It can

---

[37] Williams, *Metropolitan Political Analysis.*
[38] Lewis Mumford, *The City in History* (New York: Harcourt, Brace, 1961) chap. 16.

show why the study of urban policies cannot be simply the aggregation of policy areas and also how an ecological urban perspective can illuminate our understanding of those areas. Let us use housing and police as example.

Housing is not a single policy, but a complex of them, reflecting the fact that housing represents a bundle of values.[39] In its most basic sense, housing involves biological shelter from the elements: it defines the social space of the basic household unit and, as a large and durable consumption item, it is often a form of savings and investment. Finally, housing, through its location, provides a platform of access to the non-household world. Of this bundle of values, the latter is most singularly urban in nature, though urban conditions can affect the others as well.

The actual physical construction of housing is a production problem involving labour policy, technology and management skills. Given its importance in the G.N.P. national resource issues are often at stake, and the financing of housing involves income redistribution policy. Ultimately, national housing policy must also involve an urban policy as well, because housing need must always be defined spatially. There is unused housing available in the remote rural areas of North America and in the core areas of Eastern United States industrial cities. This 'surplus' occurs because these locations do not afford satisfactory access for those in housing need. The housing shortage always occurs in the rapid growth areas, where opportunity is greatest. When all is said and done, though national housing policy includes financing, interest rates, technology research, labour laws, tax policies and resource allocation, housing must ultimately be placed on the ground when it is built. When this happens, housing enters the realm of urban politics.

When new housing enters the urban social access world, questions are always raised about the new occupants. Predictions about who they will be, and who will pay the bills accompanying their arrival, constitute the potential political grist of urban housing politics. The issue may take the form

[39]   Wallace F. Smith, *Housing* (Berkeley: Univ. of California Press, 1971) chap. 1.

of status apprehensions and concern for the quality of the neighbourhood. It may take the form of fears about over-burdening public services, particularly school classrooms or transportation facilities. It may take the form of who will decide who gets the new housing, if government-subsidised; do 'local' people in crowded or difficult circumstances get priorities? Whatever the specifics, urban growth and change always mean an alteration of the access pattern; the neigh-bourhood will never be the same; it will lose its older iden-tity. Given these facts, the single most important variable in urban housing politics is whether citizens adjacent to new housing projects will have a substantial voice in the decisions about what will be constructed. When a local veto is exercised, the likely result is residential area segregation by status groups.

Residential segregation may take a number of additional forms, including by occupancy contract or type of structure. Rich and poor, black and white, native and foreign-born, old and young, with children and without, owner-occupied, rent or rent with subsidy, single houses or flats: these are all the issues of neighbourhood housing politics. There is rarely a single and unitary housing market. Populations with certain attributes have access only to certain types of tenure, or to certain specific housing (no kids, cats or coloureds allowed). Formal and informal stratification of the housing market profoundly affects the access opportunities of the population in each category.

Police policy has less of an urban component than housing does; still, it may be treated in a similar fashion, but it too must first be translated into more conceptual language. While the police force as a particular bureaucratic unit is common to all cultures, in fact the tasks which policemen perform vary greatly from place to place. If we wish to make com-parisons across cities, we have to pick one of these tasks and define it. The central police function is usually the protection of persons and property against dangers stemming from the behaviour of deviant actors. Obviously, the total social invest-ment in protecting persons and property from potential criminal acts is not confined to police budgets. To compare how the protection function is performed in urban areas, we need to consider many things, including investment in latch locks, barred windows, armoured trucks, private patrolment and night-watchmen, insurance policies, citizen education in use of caution, various lighting devices, burglar alarm systems and all the other paraphernalia used to create security.

How might an urban political analyst look at the inter-action between the urban system and the problem of protection from deviants? In the simplest terms, crime involves the accessibility of criminals to victims and loot. This formulation leads us to look at the propensity of a population to engage in a crime, on the one hand, and the likelihood of its happening, on the other. It cannot be assumed that there is a direct relationship between the two.

Efforts to give an urban explanation to the first of these two elements have been a major preoccupation of sociologists and social psychologists. The focus at one time was on the normlessness of urban society; it was thought that the excessive anonymity and impersonality of urban life did not teach people how to behave properly. However, if one considers the major cities of the world today, one is immediately struck by the great variance in criminal activity among them, particularly with respect to crimes of violence. Tokyo is no less urban than New York City, but it certainly is much safer. This suggests that it is hardly urbanism *qua* urbanism that creates criminals. The next step is, of course, to detail the differences among high and low crime cities, determining if these differences are urban or national in character.

It is only when we begin to try to separate out the levels of social composition along some conceptual line that we can begin to get a handle on such a problem. While it is highly improbable that the urban interaction pattern can explain the total variance in criminality, there are interesting possibilities to explore. If crime is largely learned behaviour, transmitted through peer groups and reinforced by the actions of favoured adult models within a relevant subculture, then certain neighbourhoods might, in fact, be fertile breeding grounds for criminal behaviour. It might also be true that propinquious interaction patterns create the kind of anonymity which provides opportunity for crime, for, as sight declines as a basis for interactions, strangers are less easily detected. This implies that automobile-based urban forms will have greater crime potential in the long run.

While such perspectives may not give us theoretical explanations of the causes of crime, the urban system does furnish a platform for observation. If crime is recurring and patterned, rather than random and fortuitous in the who — where sense, then we may well ask in what way the urban interaction context provides the favourable or unfavourable environment.

SUMMARY

The central argument of this article is that a spatially based conception of urbanism has advantages over other formulations in urban political analysis. It focuses on a process which is central to all settlements considered cities by scholars and laymen, without regard to time or place. Because of their importance and significance as instruments of social access, locations are objects sought with intense effort. This effort, often highly competitive in nature, gives rise to the creation of officially sanctioned rules and norms which define the permitted and the forbidden in all urban communities. The process of forming these locational arrangements and rules for governing changes in them forms a logical central focus for political analysis.

This conception of urbanism has the additional advantage of recognising that all that takes place in cities is not necessarily urban. The spatial order which is related to social access arrangements furnishes a criterion for making distinctions. These distinctions enable us to abstract a set of behaviours which are interrelated and have system properties. Spatial forms are distinctive, and the existence of one form excludes the possibility of alternatives. Changes in one part of the pattern always affect other parts. Knowledge of these relationships should lead to a more precise way of evaluating urban political arrangements.

Finally, a spatial approach to urbanism furnishes a platform for observing sets of social phenomena and determining if they are related to urbanism. Most so-called urban problems or policies are in fact influenced only in part by the existence of an urban settlement.

The ecological approach helps clarify those policy problems which are particularly derivative from urban sources. This article has stressed distributional policies which are affected by spatially based access arrangements. The city is a major value-allocating mechanism which affects who will enjoy more rewarding interactions and who less. Here, we characterise this process in terms of income, costs, opportunities and satisfactions.

A second set of considerations has more broadly public interest implications. What are the consequences for the overall urban system of giving high priorities to one set of interactions over another? For example, if homogeneous residential neighbourhoods are encouraged, so that advantaged and disadvantaged are radically segregated, does this create urban pathologies, potentially destructive responses from those who feel cut off from the presumed opportunities of urban life?

A third peculiarly urban problem is the matter of communication overload. Urbanism is a locational device to increase access to diverse others. However, escalation of this process means that there is both system and message overload. The channels and receivers cannot cope with the access efforts generated. This has long been one of the central preoccupations of urban planning, and a very correctly and properly identified one.

While there are obviously many other important policies which become apparent in cities, the question which the urban analyst asks in each case is whether the problem is a function of urbanism and the urban form or whether it exists because of the characteristics of a society generally. That societies and their cities are related is merely to repeat a truism. It is equally true that if the two cannot be distinguished, then there is no such thing as urbanism, an inference that violates the common-sense notions which impel us in the first place to inquire into the nature of cities and city politics.

'Metropology' Revisited: On the Political Integration of Metropolitan Areas

Ken Young

For many years social scientists have used the term 'metropolis' when referring to the largest urban settlements. Political scientists were for a time prominent among those scholars who studied metropolitan affairs, but the past few decades have seen the growth of urban specialisms in the disciplines of sociology, economics and geography and a corresponding decline in the contribution made by political scientists to understanding the metropolitan phenomenon. It is fair to say that much of the early metropolitan political analysis was concerned primarily with advocating the reorganisation of local government, a preoccupation eventually satirised as 'metropology', and pronounced to be 'an infantile disorder in the social sciences'.[1] Although 'metropology' has long ceased to be intellectually respectable, paradoxically its long-called-for metropolitan (or urban area-wide) authorities have now become a reality, most importantly in Toronto since 1953, in London since 1965, and elsewhere in England since 1974.[2]

*This chapter was prepared at an early stage in a research project entitled 'Political Integration in the London Metropolitan Region', supported by the Social Science Research Council.

[1]   Charles Adrian, 'Metropology: Folklore and Field Research', *Public Administration Review*, Summer 1961, pp. 148-56.

[2]   For these reorganisations, see especially H. Kaplan, *Urban Political Systems: A Functional Analysis of Metropolitan Toronto* (New York: Columbia Univ. Press, 1967); Gerald Rhodes, *The Government of London: The Struggle for Reform* (London: Weidenfeld & Nicolson, 1970); Gerald Rhodes (ed.), *The New Government of London: The First Five Years* (London: Weidenfeld & Nicolson, 1972); Donald Foley, *Governing the London Region* (Berkeley: Univ. of California Press, 1972); Frank Smallwood, *Greater London: The Politics of Metropolitan Reform* (Indianapolis: Bobbs-Merrill, 1965); Peter Richards, *The Reformed Local Government System* (London: Allen & Unwin, 1973).

The research possibilities arising from these recent developments suggest we should revisit and explore once again the politics of the metropolis, and this paper accordingly proposes the re-establishment of the politics and government of metropolitan areas as a major domain of inquiry in the field of urban politics. The structure of the essay is as follows: in the first section I argue that the concept of metropolitan character, although under attack elsewhere, still retains its utility for political analysis. The second section briefly reviews the changing perspectives in the field of metropolitan political studies during the past few decades. The third section provides a thumbnail sketch of the field of integration theory, a field which I contend has much to add to our understanding of politics in metropolitan areas. This argument is elaborated in the final section, where an analytical framework is outlined, and a tentative agenda for research drawn up.

METROPOLITAN CHARACTER AND THE 'METROPOLITAN PROBLEM'

The meaning of the term 'metropolis' is today quite widely understood, although the original usage as synonymous with an intellectual and governmental centre (literally, the 'mother city') has sadly lapsed.[3] Today we take the metropolis to mean a conglomeration of distinct communities which are bound together by their dependence upon the labour market and commercial opportunities afforded by a central city. The heart of the city, the Central Business District, is counterpointed by the residential commuter suburb, which exists to house the white-collar labour force demanded by the

[3]   The most helpful discussions of metropolitan character are to be found in Richard L. Forstall and Victor Jones, 'Selected Demographic, Economic, and Governmental Aspects of the Contemporary Metropolis', in Simon R. Miles (ed.), *Metropolitan Problems* (Agincourt, Ontario: Methuen 1970); and in Peter Hall's mammoth work, *The Containment of Urban England* (London: Allen & Unwin, 1973). For a discussion of some definitional problems, see Henry S. Shyrock Jr, 'The Natural History of Standard Metropolitan Areas', *American Journal of Sociology*, Sep 1957, pp. 163-70.

commercial and administrative organisations located at the
C.B.D. So simplified a model of course exists nowhere, the
real-life metropolis being a complex web of major sub-centres
industrial suburbs, high-density luxury areas at the urban
core, and a galaxy of other types of social area, some of them
unique even nationally and internationally.

The essence of the metropolis may nevertheless be
expressed in simply dualistic terms, as a tension between
unity in the economic sphere and *diversity* in the social
sphere. Less simply, it may be understood as a tension
between economic integration and social differentiation:[4]
with social differentiation comes political differentiation, and
the political patterns of the metropolis show a sharp and
perhaps increasing polarisation of political styles and ideologies. The conflicts which arise thereby are intensified by
one important consequence of metropolitan growth, namely
governmental fragmentation. The administration of the
metropolis is rarely under the control of a single authority,
for the burgeoning suburbs attain or increase their legal
autonomy with the result that the political conflicts of the
metropolis are typically *inter-authority* conflicts. From the
governmental aspect, therefore, we may regard the essential
dualism of metropolitan life as a tension between the needs
for area-wide administration of common services and the
forces for identity-maintaining suburban separatism. It is in
just such terms that political scientists and politicians alike
have conceived the 'metropolitan problem', for much of the
metropolitan debate is concerned with how to achieve integration in the political sphere.

Two issues of relevance to the foregoing analysis may now
be introduced. In the first place, many claim the metropolitan phenomenon (first recognised in London by H. G.
Wells in 1903[5] and responded to sixty years later) to have

---

4   Such a conception of the metropolis connects both with contem-
    porary systems concepts and with older strands of organicist social
    theory. My own focus upon complexity and interdependence owes
    a debt to Paul Lawrence and Jay Lorsch, *Organisation and Environ-
    ment* (Cambridge, Mass: Harvard Univ. Press, 1967).
5   H. G. Wells, 'A Paper on Administrative Areas', reprinted in Arthur
    Maass (ed.), *Area and Power* (Glencoe, Ill.: Free Press, 1959).

been superseded: technological, economic and social changes
have created a yet larger grouping, *megalopolis*, with the
result that the metropolitan/non-metropolitan distinction has
been rejected as no longer useful.[6] Such a criticism must be
accepted in any discussion of the patterns and dynamics of
urban growth, or of strategies for its management. But from
other perspectives the metropolis surely continues to exist as
a tighter, more cohesive, and generally continuous urban
settlement within the wider megalopolis. Moreover, whatever
the 'reality' of the metropolis, policy-making systems do
exist at the metropolitan level, either in the form of area-
wide authorities (as in England today) or in the form of
institutionalised co-operation (as in the United States),
reifying thereby the otherwise uncertain existence of the
metropolitan area.

Secondly, I would suggest that the governmental fragmentation of the metropolis is a consequence and not a cause of
the diversity of political styles, interests and ideologies that
abound in metropolitan life. From this viewpoint the 'metropolitan problem' is unlikely to be legislated out of existence.
Rather it lies in the very nature of a pluralistic (or, where
cross-cutting cleavages are absent, a *dualistic*) urban society
in which the dominant cleavage is that of social class. The
force of such a criticism of traditional 'metropology' seems
to me undeniable, but it should not be allowed to divert our
interest away from issues of metropolitan governmental
structure, or obscure the fact that alternative patterns of
government represent alternative modes of institutionalising
political conflict.

[6] For the various formulations of this point, see Jean Gottman,
Megalopolis (New York: Twentieth Century Fund, 1961); Peter
Goheen, 'Metropolitan Area Definition: A Re-evaluation of Con-
cept and Structural Practice', in Larry S. Bourne (ed.), *The Internal
Structure of the City: Readings in Space and Environment* (New
York: Oxford Univ. Press, 1971) pp. 47-59; H. J. Dyos, 'Agenda
for Urban Historians', in Dyos (ed.), *The Study of Urban History*
(London: Edward Arnold, 1968); J. Friedman and J. Miller, 'The
Urban Field', *Journal of the American Institute of Planners*, 1965,
pp. 312-19; and Hall, *Containment of Urban England.*

I propose to return to questions of conflict later in this paper, but at this stage it is worth making the additional point that, thanks to the pioneering work done by Oliver P. Williams in political science, and by David Harvey in geography, we are now also coming to recognise the function of metropolitan areas as major access-according and resource-allocating systems within the wider society.[7] If our attention is thereby turned towards the relationship between spatial location and class, status, power and 'real income', we can readily see that in the metropolis, where age and size of settlement have produced a more definite pattern of residential segregation than elsewhere, the perennial questions of politics — 'who gets what, when how?', or 'who gets *where*, when, how?' — are thrown into the starkest relief, and the 'metropolitan problem' is given a new dimension of meaning as a problem of equity.

The apparent inability of metropolitan authorities to tackle such distributional imbalances through, for example, housing and land-use policies forces us to raise certain issues, some familiar, some new: should political unity be sought merely in terms of administrative integration and arrangements for area-wide government, or can the metropolis ever be more than this, a 'supercommunity'? What would be the dynamics, limits and constraints of such *political* integration? What relationships obtain between institutional, attitudinal and behavioural factors on the metropolitan scale? Can social justice be achieved by administrative reform? These are the questions which I shall argue serve to put 'metropology' — at root the search for a *metropolity* — back upon the map of urban political studies. But before advancing a framework within which these questions may be approached, we must first look more closely at the ways in which political scientists have thought about the politics and government of metropolitan areas.

7   Oliver P. Williams *Metropolitan Political Analysis* (New York: Free Press, 1970); David Harvey, *Social Justice and the City* (London: Edward Arnold, 1973) esp. chap. 2.

CHANGING PERSPECTIVES ON METROPOLITAN GOVERNMENT

Within the metropolitan field, the perspectives of political scientists have evolved through time from a 'reformist' position based on normative premises to a more accepting and scholarly approach which sees the primary task as being to understand the metropolitan phenomenon rather than to create change within it. The reformist tradition was established around the turn of the century while subsequent decades saw a steady and substantial growth in the American interest in metropolitan reform among academics, civic leaders and businessmen, so that by the 1930s 'a national consensus existed among experts and laymen in the field that the metropolitan problem was synonymous with decentralised government', and would be solved only by the creation of large-scale, area-wide, centralised authorities. Through these and the following decades, a stable set of assumptions concerning the appropriate organisation for government in the metropolitan areas persisted, and most of the studies of metropolitan government in specific areas shared a common set of organisational premises.[8]

By the late 1950s, however, there was growing disenchantment among political scientists as reorganisation proposals were repeatedly rejected by (usually suburban) electorates, and a new emphasis came to be placed on intergovernmental co-operation. Research meanwhile underwent a visible shift from concern with the promotion of change to concern with analysing the resistance to change; voter reactions to metropolitan reform proposals were studied by survey techniques, and the findings led to a new appreciation that 'fractionated political organisation' enshrined and protected important and

---

[8]   The two most able discussions of the changing perspectives of American political scientists upon metropolitan government, upon which this paragraph recognisably draws, are: Robert O. Warren, *Government in Metropolitan Regions: A Reappraisal of Fractionated Political Organisation* (Davis, Calif.: Univ. California Press, 1966) p.196; Wallace Sayre and Nelson Polsby, 'American Political Science and the Study of Urbanisation', in P. Hauser and L. Schnore (eds.), *The Study of Urbanisation* (New York: Wiley, 1967).

widely held social values within American society.[9] The number of such studies was legion, and in time they were followed by analysis of the patterns of public policy to which governmental 'fractionation' gave rise.[10] Led by such revisionist' scholars as Edward Banfield and Oliver P. Williams, the attack on metropolitan reform prescriptions rapidly generated a new orthodoxy.

This 'revisionist' school held sway throughout the later 1960s, but was in turn succeeded by new interests in the working of the now well-established intergovernmental co-operation,[11] in the political sociology of suburbia (a field which had flourished independently of the reorientation in metropolitan studies) and in explaining the foundations and consequences of metropolitan residential segregation, a field in which only Williams among political scientists has made a substantial contribution.[12]

This last concern with explaining patterns of residential distribution and with assessing its effects on the distribution of real incomes is pre-eminently the interest of the third distinct school of writers on metropolitan affairs, who may for convenience be dubbed the 'political economists'. Al-

[9] Foremost in recognising this feature of 'fragmented' government was Edward Banfield; see especially Edward Banfield, 'The Politics of Metropolitan Area Organisations', *Midwest Journal of Political Science*, May 1957, pp. 77-91; Edward Banfield and M. Grodzins, *Government and Housing in Metropolitan Areas* (New York: McGraw-Hill, 1958). The studies which reflected the new research orientation are too numerous to list here; many of them are cited in Timothy Schiltz and William Moffitt, 'Inner City/Outer City Relationships in Metropolitan Areas: A Bibliographic Essay', *Urban Affairs Quarterly*, Sep 1971, pp. 75-108.

[10] T. R. Dye, H. Herman, Charles Liebman and O. P. Williams, *Suburban Differences and Metropolitan Policies* (Philadelphia: Univ. of Pennsylvania Press, 1965).

[11] John K. Parker, 'Co-operation in Metropolitan Areas through Councils of Government', in Joseph F. Zimmerman (ed.), *Government of the Metropolis: Selected Readings* (New York: Holt, Rinehart & Winston, 1968) pp. 324-7; Charles Harris, *Regional Councils of Government and the Central City* (Detroit, Mich.: Metropolitan Fund, 1970); Melvin B. Mogulof, *Governing Metropolitan Areas* (Washington, D.C.: Urban Institute, 1971).

[12] In *Metropolitan Political Analysis* (see above, note 7).

though the name of Warren links the 'revisionist' and the 'political economist' schools, it is Charles Tiebout who stands out as being the dominant influence. Essentially, Tiebout and his associates were attempting to define appropriate 'publics' for 'public goods' and to derive for urban government principles of bounded territoriality so devised as to minimise 'externality effects'. Their 'value-neutral' concern was to demonstrate the rationality of locational decisions, the optimising effects of governmental diversity, and the inappropriateness of metropolitan reform.[13]

The public goods theorists have recently converged with a quite independent stream of urban geography, although the convergence has occurred only at the analytical and not at the evaluative level. Thus Harvey, while agreeing that 'there are plenty of theoretical reasons . . . for expecting considerable imbalance in the availability and accessibility of resources in an urban system', adds significantly that 'there are also good reasons for anticipating that this imbalance will usually operate to the advantage of the rich and to the detriment of the poor'.[14] Harvey's analysis leads him to the claim that the *greater equality* which he seeks could be achieved by creating area-wide governments, so taking the debate on metropolitan reform back to its starting-point.[15]

It is a matter of regret that these interesting currents of thought find no reflection within the British literature on metropolitan areas, most writers in this country being firmly

[13] C. M. Tiebout, 'A Pure Theory of Local Expenditures', *Journal of Political Economy*, Oct 1956, pp. 416-24, and 'An Economic Theory of Fiscal Decentralisation', in National Bureau of Economic Research, *Public Finance: Needs, Sources, and Utilisation* (Princetown, N.J.: N.B.E.R., 1961); V. Ostrom, C. M. Tiebout and R. Warren, 'The Organisation of Government in a Metropolitan Area: A Theoretical Inquiry', *American Political Science Reviews* Dec 1961, pp. 831-42; Robert O. Warren, 'A Municipal Service Market Model of Metropolitan Organisation', *Journal of the American Institute of Planners*, Aug 1964, pp. ; Michael S. Koleda, 'A Public Good Model of Governmental Consolidation', *Urban Studies*, June 1971, pp. 103-10; Elinor Ostrom, 'Metropolitan Reform: propositions from two traditions', *Social Science Quarterly*, Dec 1972, pp. 474-93.
[14] Harvey, *Social Justice and the City*, p. 71
[15] Ibid., pp. 70, 93-4.

anchored within the reformist tradition. Concern to 'solve' the 'metropolitan problem' by forming area-wide authorities has been remarkably constant from the time of Wells and the Edwardian radicals of London's Progressive Party, through the writings of William A. Robson both before and after the Second World War, to the recent transformations under the legislation of 1963 and 1972.[16] The creation of the Greater London Council and the subsequent creation of metropolitan authorities in provincial England modelled in part on the London 'solution' mark the legislative triumph of the reformist impulse in English metropolitan affairs.

This outline sketch of the intellectual history of metropolitan political analysis has described the three major orientations within the field: reformism, revisionism and political economy. There remains, however, a minor stream of thought which flourished briefly during the early 1960s. I refer here to an attempt to chart the interactions which occur between local areas and to interpret these relationships in terms of a rather specific concept of 'integration' in which certain causal factors in the relations between areas were identified. Such interest was an extension and elaboration of work already carried out at the European level by Karl Deutsch, who was willing to encourage the application of his interactionist paradigm from international affairs to metropolitan affairs.[17] But while the potentially fruitful body of theory to which Deutsch pointed has subsequently been exploited to the full and developed on a substantial scale by other scholars working within the field of international politics, the new integration paradigm has suffered from an inexplicable neglect in the field of metropolitan politics. The next part of this paper is therefore devoted to exploring

[16] The ideological and tactical foundations of this support were, however, by no means constant. For the changes in the stances of the political parties in London in the nineteenth and twentieth centuries, see Ken Young 'The London Municipal Society, 1894-1963: A Study in Conservatism and Local Government', Ph.D. thesis (London Univ., 1973).

[17] Karl Deutsch *et al; Political Community and the North Atlantic Area* (Princeton N.J.: Princeton Univ. Press, 1957); P. Jacob and J.V. Toscano, *The Integration of Political Communities* (Philadelphia: Lippincott, 1964).

briefly the separate but related developments in international integration studies, highlighting where possible the issues and concepts which seem capable of being transferred from that field into our own.

The proposal that these questions of metropolitan politics can be understood in terms of models drawn from the international sphere is of course by no means new. William T. R. Fox delcared years ago that 'the only theory that can describe intergovernmental relation in a metropolitan community is a theory of international politics', and this dictum has been often quoted.[18] Robert C. Wood used analogies from international relations in typifying the 'garrison suburbs', while Matthew Holden, Jr is known among urbanists not least for his paper on 'The Governance of the Metropolis as a Problem in Diplomacy'.[19]

THE NATURE OF POLITICAL INTEGRATION

Political integration is in common use as a term to denote the process whereby wider communities are built from narrower at the national and international levels. Nation-building in the third world is a field of study where the term is probably already familiar to the majority of political scientists, who will understand by it a process or a programme of welding tribes, regions, ethnic minorities into a single overall unit, united by common acceptance of the new symbols of nation-hood, through 'a sense of territorial nationality which over-shadows — or eliminates — subordinate parochial loyalties'.[20] In the international sphere, increasing trade and tourism, defence pacts, penetration by multinational business organi-sations are all thought to lead to the increasing interde-pendence of formally autonomous nation-states. Here the

[18]   Quoted in Victor Jones, 'The Organisation of a Metropolitan Region', *University of Pennsylvania Law Review*, Feb 1957, p.538; quoted again in Gottman, *Megalopolis.*

[19]   Robert C. Wood, 'The Politics of Metropolitan Areas', in *Metropolitan Problems* (Madison, N.J.: Drew Univ. Press, 1963; Matthew Holden Jr, 'The Governance of the Metropolis as a Problem in Diplomacy', *Journal of Politics*, Aug 1964, pp. 627-47.

[20]   Myron Weiner, 'Political Development', *Annals of the American Academy of Political and Social Sciences*, Mar 1965, p. 52.

term 'political integration' is used to conjure up an image of
the new multinational community, of which the European
institutions are the most frequently cited and thoroughly
studied example. Deutsch and his associates suggested that
the metropolitan 'community' might be seen in much the
same light, that the relations between cities and suburbs in
particular were subject to forces analogous to those which
shape the relations between states. The plausibility of their
analysis depends not solely upon the merit of the original
proposal, but also in part upon the current state of international theory, and it is to that area that we must now turn
our attention.

We cannot unfortunately begin with a definition, for as a
recent introduction to the politics of integration in Western
Europe warns, 'if politicians have failed to define what they
mean by "integration" then it must also be said that political
scientists have not yet reached a consensus either'.[21] Neither
is it always clear whether there is in intergration theory an
implied *end-state* to be achieved, or merely a variously
defined (if barely recognisable) *threshold* above which a
community may be regarded as 'integrated', or whether
indeed all that can be said about integration is that it is a
process (like disintegration) the general direction of which
may be recognised.

Even if we accept for the moment the more persuasive
notion of political integration as a process, there is no agreement on which are the crucial elements of the process. Nor is
there agreement on the appropriate level of analysis. Where
should the investigator's interest lie: in popular opinion, in
elite behaviour, or in the performance of the integrated

[21] M. Hodges (ed.), *European Integration: Selected Readings*
(Harmondsworth: Penguin Books, 1972), p. 12; apart from
Hodges, the other works on international integration which the
reader may care to consult are: Leon N. Lindberg and Stuart A.
Scheingold (eds.), *Regional Integration: Theory and Research*
(Cambridge, Mass.: Harvard Univ. Press, 1971); Charles Pentland,
International Theory and European Integration (London: Faber,
1973); Leon N. Lindberg and Stuart A. Scheingold, *Europe's
Would-be Polity: Patterns of Change in the European Community*
(Englewood Cliffs, N.J.: Prentice-Hall, 1970), and Amitai Etzioni
Political Unification (New York: Holt, Rinehart & Winston, 1965).

system itself? Different individual integrationists have been
concerned to analyse integration at these different levels;
they also subscribe to different conceptions of what constitutes an effective integrated organisation. Owing perhaps to
the very considerable ubiquity of the word 'integration', a
working definition is then a matter of choice for each student
of the subject.

There are, then, problems of definition and operationalisation: there are also problems in the status of political
integration as 'theory'. Haas and Hodges call for the construction of an (as yet unrealised) satisfactory theory of integration capable not only of describing the process of integration
and identifying the stages within it, but also able to explain
the sequence of stages reliably enough to enable predictions
of future outcomes to be confidently made. This call seems
over-ambitious and inappropriate; indeed, given our multitude of concerns — with different levels of of analysis, with
separate casual processes, with the explanation of change at
the international, national and sub-national levels — it is
probable that any overarching theory of political integration
would be cast at so high a level of generality as to provide a
poor framework for research. But to derive middle-range
causal theory of the *dynamics* of integration is a more reasonable ambition, and it is to that issue that I now turn, in the
hope of elucidating dynamic factors common to integration
at both the international and the metropolitan level.

THE DYNAMICS OF POLITICAL INTEGRATION

Several schools of thought co-exist among integration
theorists, although there is incomplete agreement as to their
number and their labels. Pentland, in the only thorough
survey of the subject, identifies four schools, which he names
as the federalists, the pluralists, the functionalists and the
neo-functionalists. Pentland's analysis is subtle and complex,
and possibly over-schematic. Hodges' excellent review uses a
clearer and more specific tripartite framework of federalists,
transactionalists and neo-functionalists which I shall adopt
here. What understanding do these schools provide of the
dynamics of that variety of political change which is thought
to constitute 'integration'?

(i) Federalism

The assumptions of the federalist school of international theorists bear a close affinity to the concerns of the earlier metropolitan analysts, and both groups share a further common characteristic in devoting more attention to prescribing institutional structures than to explaining how such structures may come to be adopted. Integration through federalism — 'the magical institutionalisation of the many-in-one' achieved by creating two tiers of government — is the classic formula for resolving that tension between unity and diversity which is central to the metropolitan phenomenon.

In its recognition of diversity and its stress on pluralism and toleration, federalism has been described as the intellectual heritage of the American Revolution, in contrast with the centralist authoritarianism handed down from the French Revolution.[22] This ascription of ideological lineage is attractive, not least because it corresponds with the divergent currents of thought on metropolitan reform among conservatives and radicals in nineteenth- and twentieth-century London. Federalism is pre-eminently a conservative doctrine, accepting and promoting diversity. It may be adopted as a strategy for minimising resistance to governmental union (often defined in the federalist context as 'consolidation'), as is the case now in North America, or it may be chosen deliberately as a means of attaining or even enhancing diversity, as may be plausibly argued was the case with the 1963 London government legislation. When pressed to explain *how* federal institutions came about, the federalist, while admitting the strength of social and economic forces for interdependence, denies their causal significance and stresses the autonomy of politics. He directs our attention to the crucial role of individuals, the federalist hero being the visionary political leader who achieves political unification by negotiation, diplomacy and statesmanship.

The federalist recognises that the diversity of social areas finds its reflection in divergent patterns of local leadership.

[22] Pentland, *International Theory and European Integration*, pp. 157-8.

How then can the necessary catalytic leaders arise? The answer seems to be twofold: in the first place, leaders may come to reject the values of the communities who have chosen them. On this analysis, political integration requires:
first that there should be 'traitors' within each existing political community; second, that these traitors should themselves be united by norms which they hold in common; and third, that they be more skilful in seizing the reins of power and keeping them than those who have chosen to be loyal defenders of the established norms of the society.[23]

The second explanation accords the role of leadership to regional bureaucrats. Officials serving in an area-wide capacity — and in the urban field this means planners — are free from the constraints of localist sentiment, are in their professionalism more cosmopolitan in outlook, and may operate (albeit covertly) as the 'custodians' or the 'trustees' of integration.

Federalist propositions about the dynamics of change are more plausible in situations where some degree of political interaction already occurs, or some area-wide institutions already exist. As explanations of the genesis of political integration they seem far weaker. In the urban field this is perhaps not a severe limitation, for governmental reform at the sub-national level is often imposed from above, but federalism is unconvincing in its account of the dynamics of integration at any higher level of generality. Nor does it function satisfactorily at the various levels of analysis; being confined to explanation at the unit (nation-state or locality) level it has nothing to say on the forces for change at the system level, be that system one of international or of metropolitan politics; and it ignores the significance of shifts in the orientations of ordinary citizens, being exclusively focused upon the activities and strategies of elites. Weak in its analysis on these and other scores, federalism provides more a programme than a paradigm of political integration.

[23]   P. Jacob, 'The Influence of Values', in Jacob and Toscano, *The Integration of Political Communities*, p.

(ii) Transactionalism

Transactions analysis provides a sharp contrast with federalism. Transactionalists focus upon integration in terms of the social and economic relationships between communities and, being strongly influenced by cybernetic models of social processes, postulate a network of communities increasingly bound together by developments in communications technology. Their intellectual parentage may be traced to Spencer and Wells, but the leading contemporary spokesman for transactionalism is Karl Deutsch.

In its crudest forms, transactionalism may be criticised as embodying a rigorous technological determinism. The growth of transactions is said to be dependent upon advances in the scale and scope of communications, which have the effect of binding communities more closely together, eradicating community differences in a wave of homogenisation. The catch-phrases of this determinism — McLuhan's 'global village', Wells's 'delocalisation', Webber's 'urban non-place realm' — carry only limited conviction, ignoring as they do the Spencerite conception of increasing diversity as coeval with increasing unity, or Lefebvre's dictum that 'industrial society homogenises, urban society differentiates'.[24] Most transactionalists avoid this simplistic determinism; they are none the less concerned almost exclusively with underlying social forces, tending 'to by-pass questions of actor perceptions of present and future benefits, assessing instead that those will be reflected by trends in the transactions themselves'.[25]

Few transactionalists are, however, still committed to a unilinear model of progress towards integration. Rather, the mainstream argument is that rises in the level or frequency of transactions increase the salience of one community for another. To the degree that this salience is positive (that is, the transactions are viewed as beneficial) they provide a basis for inter-community co-operation. The higher the negative salience, the greater the probability of conflict, withdrawal and the disintegration of the inter-community

[24] Quoted in Harvey, *Social Justice and the City*, p. 309.
[25] Hodges, *European Integration*, p. 20.

relationship. Positive salience is generated by mutually beneficial transactions; negative salience by mutually depriving or threatening transactions. From this perspective, then, 'communications can exacerbate relations as well as improve them, and may well emphasise divergent values and expectations rather than promote common ones'.[26]

Elements of determinism none the less remain even in these milder forms of transactionalism. Firstly, actor perceptions are thought to be shaped only by the pattern of transactions, and perceptions are directly translated into behaviour. Secondly, co-operation is said to arise from positive salience, and itself further increases that salience, which itself further promotes co-operation . . . this latter is known as the 'spillover' hypothesis, in which successful co-operation in one field will lead to steady progress through extended co-operation until the threshold of unity is attained. It has, however, been decisively refuted in both the international and the metropolitan spheres. In the former there is now a common distinction drawn between 'high' and 'low' politics, the former denoting areas of activity into which co-operation is not permitted to 'spill over';[27] in the metropolitan field, Oliver P. Williams and his associates argued a distinction between 'system maintenance services' (in which all concurred in the assessment of mutual benefits) and 'life-style' services (in which co-operation was seen as leading to unwelcome 'message exchanges' and was thus rejected).[28] At this point, convergences between federalism and transactionalism begin to emerge. Definitions of 'high' and 'low' politics are shifting, and are essentially formulated by political elites who may be influenced by considerations of strategic or tactical advantage. The dichotomies between 'high' and 'low' politics, 'system maintenance' and 'life-style' services suggest as feasible a system founded on the principle of 'divided

[26] Ibid., p. 16.
[27] Roger Hansen, 'Regional Integration: Reflections on a Decade of Theoretical Efforts',*World Politics,* Jan 1969,pp. 242-71; reprinted in Hodges, ibid.
[28] O. P. Williams, 'Life Style Values and Political Decentralisation in Metropolitan Areas', *Southwest Social Science Quarterly,* Dec 1967, pp. 299-310.

sovereignty', the classic two-tier structure of federalism. Common ground exists therefore between these two other-wise divergent approaches to political integration. Insights from both schools have now been incorporated in the currently dominant third school of thought — the neo-functionalists.

(iii) Neo-functionalism

'The essence of the neo-functionalist argument is that political integration comes about less through pressures from functional needs or technological change as such, and more through the interaction of political forces — interest groups, parties, governments, international agencies — which seek to exploit these pressures in pursuit of their own interests.'[29] This school is today closely associated with the name of Haas, whose followers — most prominently Lindberg — currently rank as the most prolific writers in the field. Neo-functionalists focus not only upon the patterns of transactions between communities, but also upon the values and perceptions of political actors at both the elite and the mass level. They may be concerned with Haas to define integration in terms of an 'authority-legitimacy transfer' in favour of the larger community, or with Lindberg in terms of system performance.[30] Either way, so far as elites are concerned, the grand strategic designs of leaders are de-emphasised in favour of tactical moves by broader coalitions of leaders seeking limited advantages and exploiting socio-economic forces. In the neo-functionalist analysis, the hero is the Machiavellian who, recognising *fortuna,* can 'catch events and run with them'.

Neo-functionalism provides the more convincing account of political behaviour, and eschews a unilinear model of 'progress' for alternative scenarios of integration, equilibrium or disintegration. Neo-functionalism has also produced the

---

[29] Pentland, *International Theory and European Integration,* p. 100.
[30] See Ernst B. Haas, 'The Study of Regional Integration: Reflections on the Joy and Anguish of Pretheorising', a paper reprinted in Lindberg and Scheingold (eds.), *Regional Integration.*

more complex models of the integrative process, capable of encompassing a wide range of issue areas, of actors, of outcomes and of modes of conflict resolution. Further, it is the neo-functionalists rather than other schools who have recognised the applicability of their model at the international, national and sub-national levels.[31] Finally, in developing multi-dimensional models of integrative behaviour the neo-functionalists cope with the levels-of-analysis problem, whereby any potential theory must deal with the process of change at the system (metropolis) level, the unit (local community) level and the individual actor level.

The richness, suggestiveness and complexity of the neo-functionalist writings lead on to the conclusion that we are faced not with a choice between three competing theories (or, as Haas would have it, pre-theories), but rather that any further advances in theory are likely to take place within the comprehensive framework advanced by the neo-functionalists, who have incorporated the insights of the other two schools. It may be fairly argued that neo-functionalism is unduly speculative about such matters as elite and mass political attitudes and behaviour, but this is a defect which follows from the ambition of comprehensive explanation. Neo-functionalism is more than just a paradigm; rather it includes a range of models and propositions, some more fully worked out than others, some well tested and demonstratively valuable, some inherently testable, others in need of further development. Despite all this, neo-functionalism is among urbanists perhaps the *least* well known of the three bodies of thought. We are all acquainted with metropolitan federalism, and communications or transactionalist approaches are not unfamiliar in the urban field; what can now be drawn from the neo-functionalist writers to advance our understanding of the patterns of metropolitan political change?

---

[31]   For this, see particularly Fred M. Hayward, 'Continuities and Discontinuities between Studies of National and International Integration: Some Implications for Future Research Efforts', in Lindberg and Scheingold, ibid.

A RESEARCH AGENDA: PROPOSITIONS AND QUESTIONS

The early parts of this paper sought to delimit the metropolitan political system as a coherent domain of inquiry. The third section examined briefly some of the main currents in the field of integration theory. This final section presents a few of the questions and propositions about metropolitan politics suggested by my reading of neo-functionalism. The selection is a highly individual one, and reflects the priorities of a particular research project currently under way. Other writers would choose to focus upon other aspects of integration theory; still others will find their needs met not by imports from the international relations field, but perhaps from social psychology, the sociology of organisations, general systems theory, or from the still fresher perspectives of interorganisational theory or even operations research. With these caveats, I turn now to propose a range of hypotheses, scenarios, propositions and questions; the experienced metropolitan analyst may of course find little of substantive novelty here, but rather a reformulation (perhaps merely a resurrection?) of a familiar agenda of concerns.

The topics which I now propose to consider are chosen as being relevant to a given situational context; without wishing to tie these topics town to too specific a concrete situation, it is necessary to state the general assumptions which underlie the research setting within which this paper has been written. I assume (and this will not, I hope, deter the American reader who has followed thus far with patience) that governmental reorganisation occurs in metropolitan areas, at the behest of a higher level of government; that the institutions created conform to the federal or two-tier pattern; that national policy-makers expect the area-wide authority to tackle strategic problems of planning and communications while the second-tier authorities provide for the needs of groups of the population; and that formal powers have been distributed accordingly. I also assume that the metropolitan authority broadly represents the 'physical' rather than the 'functional' metropolis. As a result, its area includes substantial suburbs, but excludes the further-flung commuter districts. Partly because of the boundaries chosen, a state of approximate political balance obtains, whereby both the inner-city working-class party and the suburban middle-class party have a reasonable expectation of assuming control of the area-wide authority under favourable circumstances.

Working from these assumptions (which of course correspond roughly with recent events in England) there seem to be three major areas of interest in the effects of creating a new system of government upon which neo-functionalism would lead us to concentrate if we wish to assess the consequences of institutional change. They are respectively the *integrative effects,* the *distributive effects* and the *performance effects.*

(i) Integrative Effects

One approach to the assessment of integrative effects is to focus upon changes in attitudes and behaviour. Here we would be concerned with integration as a shift in the loyalties of political actors towards the new units. That shift can be expressed (following Haas) as an 'authority-legitimacy transfer' in which political actors both reorient themselves and adapt their behaviour. Integration considered from this standpoint represents a profound change in political culture, or, more accurately, in the spatial patterning of the urban subcultures. In normative and empirical terms, we are concerned with the emergence of a genuine community which we may term *metropolity.* Attitudinal and behavioural shifts may be expected to occur among political elites, and certain factors may be isolated as promoting or militating against these shifts for both elite groups and for individual leaders. We would ask whether changes occur in mass attitudes and behaviour, and whether there is increasing dissonance between the perceptions of elites and masses, and attempt to determine whether leaders or followers set the pace of change. The crucial linkages for elite — mass communications in this context need to be identified, as do those symbols of community which are mobilised in support of and in opposition to change, and their effectiveness assessed. Ultimately we should ask within what limits is the new system able to allocate values authoritatively, whether spatial variations occur, and if so how they are patterned.

A complementary approach would be to focus upon

changes in the frequency, level and intensity of *conflict*. Here
we might pose the question: what are the effects of institutional reform upon conflict? Three possible scenarios
may be outlined and their causal assumptions noted. In the
first scenario the level of conflict is *diminished*, for conflict
arises from governmental fragmentation, is exclusively intercorporate, and can be eliminated by sufficiently radical institutional change. In the second scenario the level of conflict
is *unchanged*, for conflict arises from social area differences,
which remain in the short term and are oblivious to institutional change; conflict simply moves from the inter-
authority to the intra-authority forum. In the third scenario
the level of conflict is *intensified*, for conflict arises not from
social area differences but from the *perception* of such differences; the new patterns of elite interactions which follow
the merger of separate areas raise the salience of difference,
thus realising latent conflictual situations. Which of these
scenarios is played out in the aftermath of reorganisation?

An approach which combines both the above perspectives
is one which focuses upon the effects of conflict on the level
of integration (expressed as attitudes and behaviour) itself. It
is commonplace that conflict may have either a positive or a
negative effect on integration; indeed, conflict may have an
integrative function.[32] Conflict may result in the disruption
of destruction of inter-community bonds, but may equally
well contribute to the establishment and reinforcement of
such bonds through precedent-setting and rule formulation,
or even by the process of mutual adjustment. The key
question here is to determine which conflict issues have an
integrative effect, and which a disintegrative effect. I have
suggested elsewhere that many of the conflicts which occur
in the early stages of a reorganised two-tier system are of a
temporary nature and arise from role uncertainties and
adjustments on the part of the new authorities: new procedures and institutions are created for the avoidance of such
conflicts in the future. Other conflicts are endemic in a two-

[32]   Robert C. North, Howard E. Koch Jr and Dina A. Zinnes 'The
Integrative Functions of Conflict', *Journal of Conflict Resolution*,
Sep 1960, pp. 355-74; Lewis Coser, *The Functions of Social
Conflict* (London: Routledge & Kegan Paul, 1956).

tier system; metropolitan and local interests may be in opposition, but are resolved by compromise within the context of ongoing consultation. Yet further conflicts, although still apparently intercorporate in nature, are at root *social area conflicts* and involve mutually incompatible value positions or 'policy conditions'.[33] These are zero-sum situations and unless such conflicts are deliberately avoided in future, they threaten to disintegrate the emerging metropolity.

(ii) Distributive Effects

There seem to be two separate batteries of questions that may be asked of the distributional or redistributional effects of reorganised two-level systems of metropolitan government.

(*a*) In the first place, does the mode of decision-making and conflict resolution favour the individual non-pecuniary interests of particular localities at the expense of other localities? If we consider for the moment that much of the inter-local politics in metropolitan areas is in effect the politics of housing classes, substantial numbers of citizens in favoured localities maintain or enhance their 'life chances' at the expense of members of the more deprived housing classes. Housing classes are (potentially) in a state of competition for a scarce resource — land. Does the metropolitan system work in favour of the privileged localities, or does it work to remedy the imbalances of advantage through area-wide public housing policies? Space on this analysis is both a political resource and a political value which is allocated authoritatively; within what limits can changes in spatial allocation remain authoritative and be accorded compliance? These are not questions to be answered in isolation from the broader question of the effects of inter-locality bargaining upon the overall pattern of real income distribution through locational decision-making.

(*b*) A second approach to the study of the distributive effects of metropolitan reform is to focus upon the changing patterns of fiscal burdens and monetary benefits. Much of

[33] Ken Young, 'Inter-tier Political Relations in a Metropolitan System', *Local Government Chronicle*, 9 Oct 1971.

the resistance to metropolitan reorganisation has been interpreted in terms of suburban fears of consequential increases
in tax burdens; these fears may be realised or negated. The
creation of larger authorities itself may spread tax burdens
more equably, but the overall result for changes in relative
burdens is also dependent upon the distribution of spending
powers between the two levels of government and the
variable dispositions to spend among the authorities at the
lower level. These variable dispositions may result in greater
variation in the benefits paid to individuals (for example,
welfare payments, charges for services, public housing rents)
and these variations may either diminish or increase inequities.

The analysis of both real income and monetary questions
touches upon the vital relationship between urban spatial
structure and urban social structure, and upon the processes
which maintain these structures. To paraphrase Lasswell, the
question becomes 'who gets what, where, how?'

(iii) Performance Effects

Whereas the two foregoing sections dealt with the perhaps
less familiar questions of integrative and distributive effects,
this section considers the consequences of metropolitan reorganisation for the performance of functions at the local
and area-wide levels, a question familiar to all concerned with
urban affairs, and indeed tedious to many.

Metropolitan authorities have a multiplicity of formal
tasks imposed by legislation, but the main implicit task or
rationale of the area-wide authority is to make workable
strategic policy in the fields of population, employment, land
use, location and communications. While this task may be
obscured by peripheral functions, it is by such a standard
that metropolitan reorganisation will be judged. Again, three
scenarios may be suggested here. The metropolitan system
may simply fail to perform the task of effective regional
policy-making; it may not become an effective problem-
solving agency, and in such cases it will be open — perhaps
willingly — to pre-emption or supplantation by some *ad hoc*
body. Secondly, it may reach those goals in a satisfactory
manner according to the implicit criteria of high policy-

makers. Thirdly, the system may achieve a degree of success in its original role and be able to expand and redefine that role in ways not originally expected, or redefine the means by which given ends may be attained.

Both the persistence of the system and its ability to meet goals are, however, dependant to some degree upon its ability to cope with stress from the environment: public feelings, private interests, the superimposition of other goals by national government, and influence by political parties towards non-strategic objectives. Failure to make appropriate responses to stress may lead to either the withdrawal of supports or the escalation of demands and by that route to political crisis, governmental reconstruction or the radical reallocation of functions. Here we might attempt to determine which factors operate upon system capability, in particular the significance of professionals in the metropolitan system and of varying styles of metropolitan leadership. The linkages between the metropolitan governmental system and other levels of government and other non-governmental actors may also substantially aid or constrain task performance. We might explore the images within which metropolitan elites perceive their task, and the degree to which these perceptions are shared by others at key points. It also seems possible that the agencies of political recruitment and socialisation may affect the composition of the metropolitan elite in ways that are functional or dysfunctional for the system.

CONCLUSION

This paper has presented an argument for the refocusing of interest upon the politics of metropolitan areas. A review of past literature in this field indicates that, with the exception of Williams's work, little of major theoretical interest has been carried out in recent years. A brief review of the literature in the field of integration theory suggests the applicability of integrationist concepts to the metropolitan scene. From a survey of the integrationist writings three areas have been singled out for special attention: those of the integrative effects, the distributive effects, and the performance effects.

It is this latter topic which has received most attention to date, although it may be argued that the very considerable research effort devoted, for example, to evaluating the London government reforms produced little of a conclusive nature. It may also be felt that the fruitfulness of such efforts bears no comparison with the studies of the determinants of policy discussed by other contributors to this volume.

The problems of uncovering the *distributive effects* of institutional change have received little attention from political scientists, and it seems probable at the time of writing that the main advances in this field will be made by economists and by urban geographers. It may be safely predicted that such neo-Marxist perspectives as Harvey's will generate increasing support, although metropolitan reorganisation as a research setting is unlikely to have much intrinsic appeal for these scholars.

The main thrust of this paper has been to investigate the *integrative effects* of metropolitan reforms. Although this concern reflects my own personal interests, it is also possible to argue the centrality of integrative effects in metropolitan political science, for in the above discussion of all three types of effect one question recurred: *within what limits can the metropolitan system allocate values authoritatively?* The limits are surely determined by the 'level' or 'degree' of political integration: shifts in orientations and corresponding behaviour modification are necessary conditions for altering the distribution of real income in the urban system; and in the case of task performance, one major variable is the legitimacy accorded to the metropolitan authorities in making regional policy. The three types of effect are probably interdependent: metropolitan task performance depends in the long run upon the ability to reallocate real income, which in turn depends upon the degree of political integration at the elite and mass levels. For these reasons, the new metropology might sensibly begin with the study of metropolitan political integration.

Comparative Urban Politics and Interorganisational Behaviour

Stephen L. Elkin

INTRODUCTION

Lima, Peru, has no city government. The central city is divided into several municipalities including a portion governed by Lima Province.[1] Similarly, Valencia, Venezuela, is largely governed by a variety of central government agencies over which the local authority exercises limited influence.[2] In contrast, Zagreb, Yugoslavia, has a metropolitan area government which can vote its own budgets, pass laws and establish agencies without central control.[3] In Calcutta, India, the chief executive is appointed by the state government, but locally elected councillors have considerable voice in a variety of administrative matters and personnel appointments, decisions in Calcutta reflecting these two apparently evenly balanced actors.[4] In Lodz, Poland, however, local decisions are largely made in central departments, and in conflicts between the local council and ministerial orders, the latter tend to dominate.[5]

These are all examples of city or metropolitan governmental patterns, and they and their counterparts are part of the subject-matter of the study of comparative urban politics. Yet it is not clear what each of these governmental patterns and the political behaviour associated with them have in common. What concepts can capture on the one hand a city politics in which there is either no city government or one in

---

*This paper originally appeared in *Policy and Politics*, June 1974, pp. 289-308.

[1] See Annmarie Hauck Walsh, *The Urban Challenge to Government* New York: Praeger, 1969) p. 89.
[2] Ibid. pp. 83-4. [3] Ibid., p. 146. [4] Ibid., pp. 96, 105, 114.
[5] Ibid., p. 145.

which the local authority can take few independent actions, and on the other hand a city which raises its own revenues and decides on many of its own policies? This is now a widely recognised problem in the cross-national study of urban politics. An elaboration of this problem and a discussion of a framework for an answer are the principal subjects of this paper. Particularly, some arguments from organisation theory, growing out of the analysis of interorganisational behaviour, are offered as a means of dealing with some of the principle difficulties of comparative urban political inquiry.

The simplest resolutions of the conceptual problems posed by the heterogeneity of urban political units, viz. focusing on the government of the central city or the government(s) of the metropolitan area as the unit of analysis, are generally conceded to be inadequate.[6] Likewise, delineating similarities and differences between overall patterns of governance for cities and metropolitan areas is unacceptable, as comparative statements are made impossible by the lack of common units of analysis. While these two kinds of response are clearly unsatisfactory, more substantial arguments have been made. The latter need to be discussed in more detail and their merits in coping with the various problems raised by the diversity of governmental forms considered. This forms the other principal concern of the paper and precedes the discussion of organisation theory. Where appropriate, these approaches are also assessed with regard to whether a domain of inquiry is adequately defined. Even if they do not squarely meet the problems raised here, they may be useful in providing guidance in other respects. If they are diffuse or incoherent they simply add to the difficulties generated by the diversity of governmental patterns.

6   See, for example, Robert Daland, 'Comparative Perspectives on Urban Systems', in Daland (ed.), *Comparative Urban Research* (Beverly Hills, Calif.: Sage Publications, 1969); Oliver P. Williams, *Metropolitan Political Analysis* (New York: Free Press, 1971); and Mark Kesselman, 'Research Perspectives in Comparative Local Politics: Pitfalls and Prospects', *Comparative Urban Research*, Spring 1972, pp. 10-30.

PROBLEMS IN COMPARATIVE URBAN POLITICS

The 'openness' of city politics

The first task is to analyse in greater detail the problems posed by the diversity of governmental forms in city and metropolitan areas. This variability in the units for comparison is part of a general problem; even in those contexts where governments responsible for cities or metropolitan areas possess considerable legal authority, an important property of such units is their 'openness'. Given substantial variation between cases, an important part of what is done by urban governments and how it is accomplished is dependent on factors outside the boundaries of the formal set of authority patterns that characterise the local unit, and outside the local political arena. Indeed, the very difficulty apparent in talking with precision about *local* political arenas and the legal boundaries of local units itself makes the point. This is the case even in the American context where attempts to restrict analysis to variables specific to the local arena have the greatest plausibility; increasing federal and state involvement means that for some cities in some major policy areas, more than 50 per cent of their budget is provided from outside sources. It is the fact of openness, both in a formal legal sense and in a behavioural sense, which in part sets the variability problem: when we talk about the variability of local government units we are usually referring to the varying degrees of involvement of other than local authorities in the governance of localities.

If having a local focus is unsatisfactory and we must go outside, how 'far' outside shall we go? What are the relevant sets of actors, in what terms shall they be defined, and how shall variations be conceptualised? An example will help here. The standard analysis of English and American city politics sees the former as being more open (i.e. less 'autonomous'). Variations in legal authority, central administrative controls, budgetary sources, political culture, political parties and nationally organised interest groups all work to produce the difference. What happens in English cities is more dependent on national political factors than is the case for American cities.[7] In the study of English city politics, then, particularly in some functional areas such as education, it is unclear what the unit(s) of analysis should be. To say that we need to trace out all the relevant actors at both local and national levels is satisfactory so far as it goes; but if in the same policy area in American cities a quite different set of actors is involved, on what dimensions do we compare? What concepts encompass the variation?

Closely related to the first set of difficulties is a second, viz. how to characterise the variety of relationships with actors who are 'outside' the local unit, particularly those at the central government level. If English city governments are more dependent on central agencies for a range of resources than their American counterparts, we require concepts to analyse these differences. In general, local units are often not simply passive recipients of central government largesse. But the degree of bargaining varies, as does the degree of dependence, and so a variety of types of relationship are present, running from the use of intricate strategies to extract resources which attempt to draw in attentive publics, to insulated routinised patterns, where the professional relationships of civil servants dominate the proceedings.

A third problem is that neither the openness nor the complex linkages are restricted to *governmental* actors. In the American context it is now clear that some of the more powerful actors in the politics of cities are groups of non-local citizens who form attentive publics on urban matters and to whom local politicians are sensitive, owing to their political ambitions and revenue needs.[8] In much the same way, clientele groups of central government agencies, who are either national in scope or tied to other local areas, are often powerful actors in the politics of any given city or metropolitan area. In other systems, for example in England, urban politicians give less attention to attentive publics outside

---

[7] See Howard Scarrow, 'Policy Pressures by British Local Government', *Comparative Politics*, Oct 1971, pp. 1-28; J. A. G. Griffith, *Central Departments and Local Authorities* (London: Allen & Unwin, 1966).

[8] See, for example, James Q. Wilson, 'The Mayors *vs.* the Cities', *The Public Interests*, Summer 1969, pp. 25-40.

their own constituency.[9] Analysis of citizen political behaviour in city politics requires not only concepts which encompass cross-national differences in political formations
ranging from class to tribal groupings,[10] but also concepts
applicable to the political activities of citizens who are not
within the writ of authority of the local unit under consideration.

These several problems can be brought together in the
following formulation: we require a theoretical strategy
which will enable us to analyse organisations which, while
they have defined geographic competency, much of what is
interesting about them is located outside their boundaries.
This is the case both in explaining local government behaviour and in describing its impact, which is often as great
outside the borders as inside. It is the former that is of
principal concern here. To the extent that the political
patterns we seek to explain are not influenced by such outside forces (and this requires empirical investigation), then
the arguments made here do not apply. The available
evidence suggests, however, that such 'self-contained' situations are becoming less common. The behaviours captured
under such rubrics as variability of units, openness, and
linkages to outside actors are therefore central to urban
political inquiry and likely to become increasingly so.[11]

Communities, systems and localism

Scholars whose concern with urban political phenomena has
been nurtured in the study of American cities are likely to be
tempted to utilise approaches developed in the American
context for analysis of non-American cases. The two
approaches that are most developed and therefore most likely
to be employed are the community power approach and

[9]   See Stephen L. Elkin, *Politics and Land Use Planning: The London
      Experience* (Cambridge: Univ. Press, 1974).
[10] See Daland, in *Comparative Urban Research.*
[11] Although the focus here is on cross-national comparisons, the
      argument developed is applicable to comparative work within a
      single nation. Indeed, it has been argued that these two efforts
      cannot be separated, and if this is the case, then the two kinds of
      analysis *must* share at least some concepts.

'systems' theory. Non-American cities and metropolitan areas
are studied through the prisms of communities or systems
and the concern is with the determinants of the distribution
of power or with system outputs, by which is usually meant
municipal expenditures.[12]

(i) Community Power Approach . The principal short-
comings of the community approach for cross-national research derives in large measures from the difficulty of
adequately defining community as the basis of study.[13] The
problem has long exercised social scientists concerned with
community behaviour and does not presently seem much
nearer resolution.[14] By itself this may not seem crucial; after
all, much social science proceeds without great definitional
precision. However, in the case of community theory the
deficiency is more important than usual for two reasons.
Firstly, in so far as the communities of interest are large
cities, then what counts as within the community and what
as hinterland is considerably more difficult to ascertain than
when we are dealing with small towns. Moreover, increasingly
with all communities, at least in industrial societies, behaviour within them is more and more influenced by higher
levels of government (and by an economic system whose
centres of influence are elsewhere).[15]

If community theory is designed to study relatively isolated social units, what is the advantage of trying to stretch it
to fit more complex situations? What is the interest in studying community power, when in many instances much of the
power which affects local well-being is not exercised in the

[12] See, for example, Delbert C. Miller, *International Community
Power Structures* (Bloomington: Indiana Univ. Press, 1970); J. Alt,
'Some Social and Political Correlates of County Borough Expenditures', *British Journal of Political Science*, Jan 1971, pp. 44-62.
[13] The community power literature is by now well known. See the
bibliography in Charles Bonjean *et al.* (eds.), *Community Politics:
A Behavioural Approach* (New York: Free Press, 1971).
[14] For an extensive discussion, see George Hillery, *Communal Organisation* (Chicago: Univ. of Chicago Press, 1968).
[15] See Roland Warren, 'A Note on Walton's Analysis of Power
Structure and Vertical Ties', *Southwestern Social Science Quarterly*, Dec 1967, pp. 369-72.

community or by community actors? What is required is a theoretical language that is *designed* to deal with the openness of local units.

*(ii) Systems Approaches.*A parallel criticism may be made of the application of systems theory to the study of urban politics. The usual meaning of systems theory in this regard is that political activity in an urban setting is construed as a set of institutions which 'process' resources and citizen concerns and produce a set of outcomes which in turn influence these concerns and resources. This 'system' is thought of as being surrounded by an environment in which non-political factors and the activities of other governments are placed.[16] A review of applications in the United States reveals no sustained attempt to deal with the impact of variables outside the local context.[17] There is, however, nothing in the assumptions of systems approaches which inevitably leads to a focus on the same level of aggregation; if anything, the contrary is the case. The deficiencies seem rather to spring from convenience.

Equally important, the use of systems approaches has been noticeable for the low level of conceptualisation, particularly as concerns environmental variables. For the most part, the environment has been conceived of as the resources available to the system and the demographic characteristics of the population, the latter usually being interpreted as measuring demands for public services or 'objective need'. The results of

[16]   See, for example, Robert Lineberry and Ira Sharkansky, *Urban Politics and Policy* (New York: Harper & Row, 1971) esp. chapter 1. For more general discussions, see David Easton, *A Framework for Political Analysis* (Englewood Cliffs, N.J.: Prentice-Hall, 1965); and Walter Buckley, *Sociology and Modern Systems Theory* (Englewood Cliffs, N.J.: Prentice-Hall, 1967). Other examples of systems approaches to urban politics can be found in Thomas Dye, 'Governmental Structure, Urban Environment and Educational Performance', *Midwest Journal of Political Science*, Aug 1967, pp. 353-80; and Noel T. Boaden, *Urban Policy-making Influences on County Boroughs in England and Wales* (Cambridge: Cambridge Univ. Press, 1971).

[17]   Lineberry and Sharkansky, in *Urban Politics and Policy*, devote 11 of their 362 pages to 'Horizontal Intergovernmental Relations', and even this small amount is largely descriptive.

such analysis are often not very edifying since we find either the obvious (for example, that wealthy systems spend more) or we search for *ad hoc* explanations (for example, of why high levels of poverty fail to lead to higher expenditures).[18] Such problems are likely to multiply when we move into non-American contexts.[19] The interpretation of association or lack thereof between these environmental variables and outcomes will be more difficult because a fund of political lore about the local communities is not likely to be so readily available. Conceptualisations of environmental variables that go beyond the simpler resource and demand conceptions and, particularly, take into account factors at higher levels of aggregation[20] might produce stronger and more comprehensible associations. At this point the systems approach seems more metaphor than theory, and although amply suited for dealing with openness and related questions, in practice it has not proved satisfactory in this regard.

It is also worth noting that at present systems approaches in urban politics are unsatisfactory because the conceptualisation is often at so high a level of generality that in practice concepts seem to be headings for a lengthy list of variables and little else.[21] Such system theorists start with concepts whose scope is so broad as to encompass an enormous range of empirical exigencies which means that the concepts lack any cutting edge. As the opening examples suggest, there is a real problem being addressed since the range of phenomena to be encompassed is in fact quite diverse. However, it cannot

---

[18]   See the comment by Robert Salisbury that it is system resources which matter in explaining policy outputs: 'The Analysis of Public Policy: A Search for Theories and Roles', in Austin Ranney (ed.), *Political Science and Public Policy* (Chicago: Markham, 1968) p. 163. See also the attempts by Robert Lineberry and Edmond Fowler, 'Reformism and Public Policies in American Cities', *American Political Science Review*, Sep 1967, pp. 701-16, to explain the pattern of their findings.

[19]   See, for example, Boaden, *Urban Policy-making Influences.*

[20]   See below for some caveats concerning this term.

[21]   See, for example the efforts by Ira Sharkansky, 'Environment, Policy, Output and Impact: Problems of Theory and Method in the Analysis of Public Policy', in Sharkansky (ed.), *Policy Analysis in Political Science* (Chicago: Markham, 1970).

be said that it is being surmounted. The same danger found in a systems approach is evidenced in accounting schemes where 'cultural' and 'structural' variations in urban politics are enumerated.[22] When, and if, general systems theory is developed further, it seems likely that there will be considerable convergence between it and the kind of organisation theory outlined below. Both are concerned with the interaction between behaviour inside and outside the focal actor.

(iii) 'Local' politics A third possible route is to merge the study of city and metropolitan politics with a general analysis of local politics. Much of the literature on city politics implicitly takes this view. In the absence of some explicit theoretical argument pointing to some other set of problems, the studies can either be construed as contributing to some general analysis of local-level politics, or they can be said to have no theoretical interest at all.[23] A principal danger here is that a theory of local-level politics which encompassed the full range of political behaviour at the local level would not be a single theory at all, but at best a set of theories about different aspects of political behaviour or at worst a collection of disparate propositions. An additional step is required in which behaviour occurring in a local context is distinguished from behaviour which has some peculiarly local-level character. The former gives us no clue as to what basis to compare; virtually all political behaviour is open to us. On what basis might the distinction be made?

If 'local' political behaviour means anything, it surely must refer to behaviour which is somehow shaped by locale. The existence of political organisations designed to advance the interests of territorial units, and the shaping of such organisa-

---

22 See, for example, Robert Alford, 'Explanatory Variables in the Comparative Study of Urban Politics and Administration', in Daland (ed.), *Comparative Urban Research.* Alford attempts to integrate the findings of several studies of urban political phenomena under these (and several other) headings.

23 See the more sophisticated effort by Donald B. Rosenthal and Mark Kesselman, 'Local Power and Comparative Politics: Notes Toward the Study of Comparative Local Politics', paper delivered to the American Political Science Association, Sep 1972. Rosenthal and Kesselman try to tie the analysis of local political phenomena to the analysis of political development.

tions by a political culture particular to the territory, combine to suggest the importance of concentrating on locale.[24] This concern with political behaviour which varies by territory is important, and in any given city or metropolitan area it may be central, but it does not open up any obvious way to deal with the *governance* of localities. Here, as already suggested, the notion of 'local' has little weight: the diversity of local governmental patterns belies any content. In short, a local politics approach will not take us far enough if we take 'local' seriously as a concept and carefully delimit the concept; if we do not, it takes us too far by opening up all political behaviour in a local context.

Urbanism, space and politics

The preceding approaches to the study of urban politics attempt to analyse the salient features of the phenomenon by emphasising similarities to other types of political behaviour. An alternative method of proceeding is to search for characteristics of urban politics that are presumed to be particular to it. This might be called an essentialist approach. In this view, which contains several possible variations, the concept 'urban' is taken seriously and questions are raised about the boundaries of the behaviour denoted by it and about political patterns linked to the urban process.

(i) Variations on the Essentialist Theme. The theme of the essentialist approach is that the dimensions of urbanism are best understood by considering the range of behaviour associated with the use of land and the various processes whereby it is allocated and distributed. Setting the dimensions of urban *politics* then becomes an attempt to isolate political patterns which are regularly associated with urbanism however defined. From this starting-point at least two tacks are possible, which need not be mutually exclusive. Firstly, an attempt might be made to define patterns of land usage and look for political patterns that are characteristic of the various contexts. Urban politics would then be that set of political patterns that are particular to the spatial arrange-

[24] See Rosenthal and Kesselman, ibid.

ments defined as urban; different political patterns are
associated with different spatial arrangements. The pertinent
question here is why such an association should be expected.
What reasons do we have to expect that the differing land-use
patterns will actually produce different political forms?[25]
Perhaps it might be argued that communication processes
differ substantially by land-use patterns; that view partly
underlies arguments about the greater ease of organising mass
movements in urban as compared with rural settings. However, since face-to-face contact is only a small portion of the
total flow of communication, the force of this approach
is weakened. There may be aspects of political behaviour
that are crucially influenced by the spatial context in which
they take place, but discussion presently available on these
matters does not inspire confidence and thus it is difficult
to think of an area of inquiry built on this perspective.[26]

The second tack is broader in its implications. In this view,
spatial patterns are seen as the outcome of a variety of forces
including technology, the market and political decisions. In
its most refined version, the advantages conferred by
different locations are seen as instrumental to the achievement of a range of social values. The political processes that
help shape the distribution of locational advantages are
seen as the subject-matter of the study of urban politics;
the numerous political forces surrounding how location is
used and by whom, from population policies to zoning

[25]   See the discussion by Z. Mlinar and H. Teune, 'The Wealth of Cities
and Social Values', *La Ricerca Sociale* (Bologna, 1972),pp. 3 - 20,
where some suggestions are offered in this regard, and the paper by
Robert Warren and Louis F. Weschler, 'Governing Urban Space:
Non-territorial Politics', delivered to the American Political Science
Association, Sep 1972.

[26]   It might be objected that suburban political behaviour is an important example to the contrary. However, while it may well be
true that suburban political agendas differ from those in the central
city, this does not mean that suburban political formations or
styles are distinctive. The same type of behaviour can be observed
in other spatial contexts.

laws to neighbourhood groups, become the focus of inquiry.[27]

(ii) Critique of the Locational Politics Approach . What is
isolated here is an allocation and distribution process for an
important instrumental value. By itself this justifies our
attention; who gets the most valuable spatial locations, how
and why, and the outcomes which result are clearly matters
of interest. And these subjects can be investigated on a cross-
national basis. There is an outcome which is common to the
various systems and which varies, and a set of processes that
seems likely to account for some of the variation. However,
what is unclear is the extent to which the allocation and
distribution of location needs to be studied in a different
manner from the study of other valued outcomes. That is,
can it be claimed that a 'distinct' social and political process
has been isolated?[28] This claim can be sustained only if it can
be shown that an understanding of the allocation and distribution of locational values requires concepts specific to the
process; or if it can be demonstrated that there is a clustering
of observations on variables that might be appropriate for the
universe of allocational and distributional processes. Otherwise it is hard to see what the value of talking about an *urban*
politics might be, as distinct from the study of the allocation
and distribution of other goods. There seems no obvious way
to resolve this issue, aside from considerable investment in
empirical work which as yet has not appeared.

The preceding argument can be extended. If the particular
characteristics of allocation and distribution of space are not
clearly demarcated from the allocation and distribution of
other valued outcomes, so eroding the boundaries of *urban*
inquiry, similarly the distinction between what affects spatial

[27] See Williams, *Metropolitan Political Analysis*. The whole literature
on land-use politics and planning is pertinent here, although the
overwhelming portion of it is not aimed at delineating an urban
political process. See, for example, Martin Meyerson and Edward
C. Banfield, *Politics, Planning and the Public Interest* (Glencoe, Ill.:
Free Press, 1955); Alan Attshuler, *The City Planning Process*
(Ithaca, N.Y.: Cornell Univ. Press, 1965); and Elkin, *Politics and
Land Use Planning.*
[28] See Williams, *Metropolitan Political Analysis*, esp. chaps. 2 – 3.

outcomes and what does not is difficult to draw. Almost the full range of social and political activity has a spatial component in so far as the activity takes place in *some* location and affects the value attached to that location. Behaviour ranging from the pattern of neighbourhood child-rearing to the amount of discretion given to police officers affects the value any actor is likely to attach to being located in a particular place. While these may not be a part of the process whereby location is distributed, in order to understand the process we need to know something about why some locations are valued over others, if only to be able to predict changes in the strategies and demands of those seeking particular locations. If the range of behaviour turns out to be as wide as just suggested, then it is not clear what may be gained by the focus on location. Although this is a common difficulty in theorising (everything is related to everything else), still, some guidance needs to be offered preferably arising out of empirical work. How far do we need to go before we call a halt?

Along similar lines, it is unclear within any given national system whether there is one urban process and thus one urban politics which is best studied as a whole, or whether intra-system distinctions are necessary and possible. Again, this is a common problem, but in this case the danger is that, without some guidelines based on theoretical considerations, because of practical exigencies we shall end up studying allocation and distribution of location in metropolitan areas defined as census categories in a formal-legal sense, thereby falling into the trap that the attempt to give theoretical coherence to urbanism was designed to avoid, namely the use of definitions which, while convenient, are not stable units of inquiry across nations.

While the preceding problems are serious, from the perspective of the present discussion, the principal drawback of the spatial approach is the lack of any explicit attempt to deal with the set of problems discussed under the heading of openness. As with a systems perspective, there do not seem to be any inherent conceptual barriers to doing so, as there are in the community politics approach, and the gap seems to be largely a consequence of where effort has been concentrated until now. These problems are central matters to any analysis of the impact of political variables on locational patterns. Some substantial part of the explanation of variation in the latter is likely to turn on the impact of actors outside the locale, and conceptualisation of such behaviour in its various dimensions will be required for satisfactory theory.

THE POTENTIAL OF ORGANISATION THEORY

A useful image in capturing the openness of city politics is that of a network of governmental organisations having as its focus the local territorial unit. The level of interdependence is relatively high between organisations in the network as compared with that between these organisations and other actors. The latter can be counted as part of the network's environment (which includes actors with which there is some interdependence and interaction and others with which these characteristics are largely absent, and which are therefore part of the distant environment). Among the former are included citizen groups, political parties and other local governments (these, of course, may be found in the distant environment as well). Beyond this, we may think of each of the organisations as having a domain, a sphere of competence, which they seek to protect or expand.[29] The extent of the domain depends to an important degree on the acquiescence of the other organisations in the network as well as acceptance by various citizen groups. The point of departure in the analysis of the network may be any of the organisations composing it, but if our concern is with city or metropolitan politics, this will usually be an actor whose primary responsibility is for these territorial units. Depending on our purposes, this may be an agency within a larger authority, or the

[29] See James D. Thompson, *Organisations in Action* (New York: McGraw-Hill, 1967) chap. 3.

authority itself.[30]

Each of the organisations in the network may be said to be seeking autonomy;[31] however, they are not autonomous but in varying degrees interdependent and it is the management of this dependence on others in the network that is of central interest.[32] It is the formal-legal situation which initially requires dependence — some actors work through others and some get part of their resources from others — but little in the way of actual relationships can be deduced from the formal arrangements. Characterisations of central/local government patterns along dimensions of hierarchy and dominance, even going beyond formal aspects, are likely to be insufficiently differentiated and too static to capture the complexity of the relationships at issue. Dependence varies

[30] This formulation hides some real difficulties. As organisation theorists have long recognised, it is not always clear what is to be counted as included in an organisation, especially when it is part of a larger one: James March and Herbert Simon, *Organisations* (New York: Wiley, 1958). For present purposes, this problem is not a pressing one; we can follow Guetzkow and 'define organisations by denotation, allowing our empirical analyses then to determine how the phenomenological entities that we use in common speech have empirical existence ...': Harold Guetzkow, 'Relations among Organisations', in Raymond Bowers (ed.), *Studies on Behaviour in Organisations* (Athens: Univ. of Georgia Press, 1966) p. 14. In some contexts, considerable sharing of personnel and tasks between organisations may require us to create a new level of analysis, which may encompass at least the range of interacting government agencies. Kronenberg argues that such an entity can be labelled an 'interorganisation' and can serve as a unit of analysis in much the same manner as the single organisation: Philip Kronenberg, 'Interorganisational Behaviour', unpublished paper (Dept. of Political Science, Indiana Univ. 1970). Should the assumption that we shall be able to talk about relations between organisations prove erroneous for the urban context, one response would be to adopt Kronenberg's perspective.

[31] See Alvin Gouldner, 'Reciprocity and Autonomy in Functional Theory', in Llewelyn Gross (ed.), *Symposium on Sociological Theory* (Evanston, Ill.: Row, Peterson, 1959).

[32] See William Evan, 'The Organisation Set: A Theory of Interorganisational Relations', in James D. Thompson (ed.), *Approaches to Organisational Design* (Pittsburgh: Univ. of Pittsburgh Press, 1966); and Thompson, *Organisations in Action*, chap. 3.

by type of resource and for different task areas. Strategies are pursued and relationships shift. And while the descriptions of some of the actors as 'local' and some as 'national' is a useful linguistic convenience and will be resorted to here, it says little about the attributes and relationships of the organisations.

As William Evan notes, the 'phenomena and problems at issue in this analysis of relations between organisations are part of the general class of boundary-relation problems confronting all types of social systems'.[33] The premise of the interorganisational approach is that organisational processes cannot be adequately explained except for reference to the impact of actors outside the organisation. This insight is common fare in the social sciences, being central to such lines of inquiry as political integration,[34] social conflict,[35] and the interaction between interest groups and administrative agencies,[36] but conceptual development has proceeded furthest in the study of formal organisations and the concepts developed in the latter literature are particularly suitable for dealing with the issues set out in the opening discussion. A review of some of the insights and propositions that may be built up from this view will suggest the potential for dealing with the enumerated problems.

Strategies to manage dependence

As suggested, the starting-point in this kind of analysis is the focal organisation[37] and its management of dependence on the other organisations with whom it deals. This management has as its purpose the protection or expansion of the focal organisation's domain. The organisation seeks to ensure that

[33] Evan, ibid., p. 175.
[34] See, for example, Philip Jacob and James Toscano (eds.), *The Integration of Political Communities* (Philadelphia: Lippincott, 1964).
[35] See, for example, Lewis Coser, *The Functions of Social Conflict* (Glencoe, Ill.: Free Press, 1956).
[36] See, for example, David Truman, *The Governmental Process* (New York: Knopf, 1951).
[37] Evan, in Thompson (ed.), *Approaches to Organisational Design*, introduces and defines this term.

it continues to perform its functions at their present level, or seeks to add to the level of performance or number of functions, each of these requiring acquisition of a variety of resources ranging from those of a material kind to prestige.[38] In its most general aspect, management requires coping with uncertainty and threat in the dependence relationships.

Given the general concern to manage dependence, it is helpful to distinguish between organisations for which this is a constant and intense focus, as compared with those for whom the problems are intermittent and require little investment. In short, it is useful to distinguish various states of the dependence relationship. Dynamic, conflictual relationships will require constant management, while stable routine ones will not.[39] Any set of interdependent organisations may have a mixture of the two. The politics of large American urban areas would appear to be closer to the dynamic, conflictual end of the spectrum than the relationships which characterise the English situation.[40] American city governments, and agencies within them, devote more resources to managing dependence and, in general, to shoring up their domains than do their English counterparts.

Focal organisations have a variety of strategies open to them to manage dependence. In highly stable and routinised states, deliberation and persuasion are likely to be the dominant mode of interaction..For the more dynamic and conflictual states the strategies include both those which involve other organisations in the network and those which also involve

---

[38] A complete analysis of the behaviour of the focal organisation, and of interdependence in the network, would require consideration not only of dependence or 'input' relationships, but those on the output side and the latter's impact on the former. The concept of the domain (of the focal organisation, and of other organisations in the network) focuses on the output dimension, but not all outputs are encompassed in a consideration of organisational tasks, nor, clearly, are the recipients of the outputs confined to formal organisations.

[39] It is important to distinguish between the overall state of dependence relationships for the focal organisation and the state of particular ones. The analysis here can apply to either, but the following discussion is particularly concerned with the former.

[40] See Elkin, *Politics and Land Use Planning*.

environmental actors.[41] We may distinguish the following:

(i) *Coalition*. The focal organisation attempts to join with others, for example to make the provision of some resource more predictable.

(ii) *Co-optation*. The focal organisation attempts to incorporate into its own decision-making structure the organisation on whom it is dependent, so as to assure regular support for its activities.

(iii) *Exchange*. The focal organisation attempts to bargain with the organisation on whom it is dependent. Each may offer an increase in some resource or an increase in the reliability of its provision.

(iv) *Penetration*. The focal organisation attempts to penetrate the organisation on whom it is dependent, usually by trying to introduce some of its own personnel into the latter. This is the reverse of co-optation.

(v) *Socialisation of conflict*. The focal actor attempts to widen the scope of conflict by involving previously uninvolved parties who, hopefully, will favourably alter the balance of opinion and resources confronting the organisation dispensing the resource.

(vi) *Setting up or making use of a supra-organisation*. The focal organisation attempts to shift the arena of decision to one in which it is more favoured. This may be done by shifting the decision to an already existing organisation in which the focal actor and the other organisation are 'members' or working towards setting up such an arena. Attempts to socialise conflict may themselves result in the arena of decision-making being shifted, and in general the last two strategies are likely to be associated.

At the same time as the focal organisation attempts to manage its dependencies by employing one or more of the above strategies, other organisations in the network are similarly engaged. The consequence is that behaviour within the network is complex and dynamic: there are multiple, overlapping relationships, each one of which is to a greater or

[41] The strategies are derived from the following: Thompson, *Organisations in Action;* Guetzkow, in Bowers (ed.), *Studies on Behaviour in Organisations;* and E. E. Schattschneider, *The Semi-Sovereign People* (New York: Holt, Rinehart & Winston, 1960).

lesser degree dependent on the state of the others. Moreover, since each organisation is likely to have a somewhat different array of relationships, i.e. interdependance is not likely to be complete or exclusive, behaviour within the network is likely to depend to some degree on that in other networks.

As noted, the most important factor affecting the use of the strategies is the general state of relationships within the network, i.e. the mixture of stability, routineness, dynamism and conflict. In the context of urban politics, we need to inquire into the variables which are likely to account for such states and thereby into the levels of investment in managing dependence by any local actor. Some of the important variables here concern the socialisation and recruitment of officials of the various governmental organisations. If officials are recruited from a common pool (defined by socio-economic characteristics), serve in more than one organisa-tion at a time (most likely for elected officials) and go through a similar training (most likely for bureaucrats), relationships in the network are likely to be more routine and stabilised because differences in values are likely to be less than where these factors do not hold. The French situation appears to be closer to this portrayal than the American, especially with regard to elected officials holding posts at various governmental levels and to the training of civil servants.[42]

Resource characteristics and strategies

The degree to which strategies to manage dependence are salient will also depend on the resource characteristics of the focal organisation. At any given time the focal organisation has a pool of resources it may invest in pursuing the various strategies. Its ability to do so successfully depends not only on the *level* of resources available, but on the *skill* with which they are utilised and the *rate* at which they may be converted into forms that are useful for a particular strategy.[43] These

42   See the discussion in Annemarie Hauck Walsh, *Urban Government for the Paris Region* (New York: Praeger, 1967).

43   James S. Coleman, *Resources for Social Change* (New York: Wiley, 1971), and Robert Dahl, *Who Governs?* (New Haven: Yale Univ. Press, 1961) chaps. 19-26, discuss conversion of resources and other aspects of a theory of social resources.

factors not only help to determine success, however, but also the extent to which any strategy may be pursued in the first place. Both these are also affected by whether the focal organisation is dependent on a single organisation for any resource which is necessary for its operations, or whether alternatives are present. If the former is the case, it will be reluctant to pursue any course in its other interactions that will jeopardise the dependence relationship.[44] This suggests that the important feature of local government financial dependence is not how much of its revenue comes from outside, but the number of alternative sources. Although American city governments have had increasingly larger shares of their operations financed through subventions from state and central government, neither their investment in complex strategies nor the size of their domains seem to have markedly diminished. Multiple sources of finance remain; indeed, the number may have increased.

Choice of strategies.

In addition to explaining the general use of strategies to manage dependence, we need also to explain the choice of *particular* strategies, or mixes thereof, by local units. In the absence of any solid data it is difficult to be precise here, but a useful starting-point is to distinguish between variables specific to the organisation and environmental variables.[45]

---

[44]   Richard M. Emerson, 'Power Dependence Relations', *American Sociological Review*, Feb 1962, pp. 3-40.

[45]   The characteristics of the network constitute a third set of variables: Evan, in Thompson (ed.), *Approaches to Organisational Design;* William Evan, 'An Organisation Set Model of Interorganisational Relations', in Matthew Tuite *et al.* (eds.), *Interorganisational Decision Making* (Chicago: Aldine, 1972). Evan points to three characteristics of interest:size, diversity and configuration. The latter refers to the types of links between organisations in the set, e.g. dyadic *vs.* 'wheel' relationships. A fully elaborated theory of interorganisational relationships would involve statements about focal actors, properties of the set, and properties of the environment of the set. See also the comments above on the general state of relationships within the network. It may also be necessary to look at characteristics of personnel who occupy boundary-spanning roles, i.e. the individual actors who mediate relationships between organisations.

The former include the resource position of the organisation as well as organisational dimensions such as concentration of influence, formalisation and specialisation.[46] The latter are concerned with the environment of the network and include such variables as the extent to which citizens are organised, and the extent to which such organisations are focused on national or local concerns. Some examples of propositions will help here.

Organisations with limited resources are more likely to attempt to manage dependence through coalition, penetration and trying to push the problem up to an existing supra-organisation rather than through co-optation, exchange or trying to build a supra-organisation.[47] Aside from coalition, which is attractive to low-resource organisations for obvious reasons, the other two strategies are likely to be favoured by such organisations because in pursuing them the level of resources is less important than the possession of a *particular* skill or resource. Examples of the latter are skill at presenting arguments before a court, or members who have the requisite talents required to join or be elected to the organisation providing the resource. The last three strategies depend on the level of resources of the focal organisation in the following senses : a high resource level defines an organisation attractive to another party (co-optation); multiple inducements are more likely to be available (exchange); slack resources are more likely to be available which may be put in long-term investments (building a supra-organisation). On the basis of this proposition we might make the simple prediction that revenue-sharing in the American context will reduce the incidence of coalitions among cities in dealing with state legislatures and increase the prevalence of exchange with the latter by individual cities.

[46]   See, for example, Derek Pugh *et al.,* 'Dimensions of Organisational Structure', *Administrative Science Quarterly,* Mar 1968, pp. 65-105.

[47]   The choice of socialisation of conflict may depend less on resource position and more on the success of other strategies to manage dependence; if they fail, then other actors are 'invited' to participate. Socialisation of conflict is likely to be a last resort because the focal organisation has relatively little control over who will respond; the other strategies offer somewhat greater control.

The lower the concentration of influence within the focal organisation, the more likely socialisation of conflict is to be utilised. The reasoning here is that an organisation with multiple centres of influence is likely to have more difficulty reaching decisions on how to manage a dependency relationship that affects the organisation as a whole than one where influence is concentrated.[48] One pattern likely to appear in attempts to reach an organisational decision will be that conflicting actors inside the organisation will turn to outside allies for support. In American cities, involving citizen groups in decisions about how to deal with state or federal involvement is common. In England, where the structure of influence within local governments is more concentrated, socialisation of conflict happens less often.[49]

Turning to the environment, the network of governmental actors which has as its focus the local territorial unit is embedded in a group of governmental and non-governmental actors, who may be drawn into attempts by the focal organisation to manage its dependencies. We would expect, for example, the use of socialisation of conflict to vary in response to the manner in which attentive publics are organised. Here we are particularly concerned with these publics, but it may be useful to think in terms of variables which characterise the behaviour of environmental actors as a whole (at least those with whom the focal organisation has some interaction). Consideration of broad environmental properties, such as the level of certainty or threat, would bring the analysis of the context of organisational networks within the general framework of environmental theory.[50]

[48] The formulation is meant to exclude those relationships that can be handled by different sectors of the organisation without major impact on other sectors. In such cases, low concentration of influence would not have the effects discussed here.

[49] See Elkin, *Politics and Land Use Planning*.

[50] See the following: Thompson, *Organisations in Action;* Paul Lawrence and Jay Lorsch, *Organisation and Environment* (Cambridge, Mass.: Harvard Business School, 1967); Tom Burns and G. M. Stalker, *The Management of Innovation* (London: Tavistock, 1961); William Dill, 'Environment as an Influence on Managerial Autonomy', *Administrative Science Quarterly*, 1962, pp. 404-33; and John Child, 'Towards a Theory of Organisation, Environment and Performance of Work Organisations', unpublished paper (London Graduate School of Business, 1970).

With regard to attentive publics, a crucial characteristic is the extent to which their membership and focus is national in scope.[51] Whether a local government tries to manage its dependence on national agencies by socialising conflicts will clearly depend on whether allies are present who are attuned to problems within its territorial responsibility or whether the organisation of the citizenry is such that their focus is on national policy. There is considerable variation across national systems in the level and kind of interest group activity in this respect, ranging from the American situation, where there is a mixture of types or organisations, to the English case, where nationally oriented groups dominate.[52] In cases of the last type, attempting to widen the scope of conflict has the clear danger that those who will respond are unlikely to look kindly, for example, on attempts by local units to expand their domains by increasing their regulatory powers. Such attempts will activate groups whose principal concern is to see that their local members get treated uniformly. Where such groups are the most numerous, local governments may be expected to favour strategies such as co-optation or penetration which are more private in character. In this whole area the difficult problem may not be how the characteristics of contextual actors affect behaviour within the network. At least at this early stage of investigation this seems reasonably straightforward; the analysis turns on who are likely to be sympathetic allies. A more interesting problem might well be how to explain variation in the types of contextual actors.[53]

Some limits on the interorganisational approach

While the organisational concepts discussed here, and the propositions built from them, provide an analytical platform for the analysis of the openness of city politics, they do not

[51] Other characteristics would include those attributes which help explain their ability to command the attention of government, including size, leadership skill, etc. See, for example, Harry Eckstein, *Pressure Group Politics: The Case of the British Medical Association* (London: Allen & Unwin, 1960).

[52] See Elkin, *Politics and Land Use Planning*, chap. 5.

[53] See the discussion in Elkin, ibid., chap. 5.

provide a complete vocabulary. For instance, it can be argued that the focus on dependence and its management is not broad enough. To balance this, however, it should be emphasised that the management of dependence is in the service of protecting and expanding an organisational domain. And the latter concept directs our attention to a wide (but not complete) range of governmental activity. When we add to this the fact that the focal organisation is part of an organisational network and that the sources of behaviour of the latter reach quite widely, then the narrowness of focus seems less so. For example, although we have focused on how the focal organisation might make use of non-local attentive publics, the analysis can be extended by considering how the latter's behaviour and preferences indirectly affect the former through their impact on other organisations in the network.

On the other hand, it must be noted that the concepts presented do not exhaust the full sources of dependence of city governmental organisations. Mention need only be made of revenue raised through local taxation. Since the focus has been on relations between organisations, those with the general citizenry have not been adequately conceptualised. To some degree, the concepts discussed do provide guidance here; we could analyse the relationships with any citizen organisations or political parties which are instrumental in generating support for local tax policies. And should the relationships between such groups and governmental organisations be continuing and intensive, they might well be treated as part of the organisational network. However, where dependence is not easily fitted into an interorganisational context, then concepts and propositions additional to those discussed here are required.[54]

---

[54] The earlier comments concerning the focus on 'input' relationships (note 39 above) also suggest a limitation in the vocabulary presented. With regard to limitations, the treatment of the openness of cities largely in terms of governmental decision-making should be noted. Clearly, cities are open social systems in more respects than this, and any comprehensive urban theory would consider such matters as economic linkages, migration patterns and diffusion of innovations.

The preceding remarks should make clear that the units of analysis and attendant concepts suggested by an interorganisational focus are not meant to be exhaustive of those that may be required for a comprehensive understanding of city politics. It is not necessary to make such a claim in order to argue, as is done here, that such units and the analysis built on them are central to such an understanding.

Given the generality of the analysis of relationships between organisations, the perspective presented here is clearly not particular to *urban* politics, as opposed to the politics of other types of localities. Again, the question of the possibility of a distinct urban political theory is relevant. Depending on how that question is answered, the absence of a distinction will or will not be acceptable. In general, abstract questions concerning whether we have exhausted the relevant units of analysis or whether there is a distinction between urban and local politics are less fruitful lines of inquiry, given our present knowledge, than the strategy of trying to disentangle the conceptual issues which arise from the diversity of political practices in the complete range of cities.

The last point warrants additional emphasis. The discussion has proceeded from what appears to be the most salient facts about the politics of cities seen in cross-national perspective, viz. considerable variation in patterns of governance and the openness of the local political arenas. The approach has been to tie these facts to bits of reasonably well-developed theory which are expressly concerned with boundary problems, openness and related matters. The informing notion has been that theory adequate to an understanding of cross-national urban political phenomena will best be constructed by attacking the specific and knotty conceptual problems isolated here, and *then* searching for an overarching theoretical orientation, if one is possible or desirable. Approaches which proceed either from a highly general theoretical perspective, for example systems theory, or whose concern is to define a general field of inquiry, i.e. to isolate an urban or local politics, are valuable in so far as they provide overall direction. But aside from the inconsistencies in some of these general positions, which have been briefly discussed above, and aside from a largely unexamined faith that some single theoretical position is appropriate for under-standing the politics of cities, the critical issue is, again, that any of these approaches must somehow handle the problems that have been isolated here. And they have not in fact done so. To this point should be added the possibility that the analysis offered here may well be compatible with one or more of these approaches, so that we may only be dealing with a division of labour problem in which intellectual styles will determine who works on what.

CONCLUSION

An interorganisational perspective provides a language to handle some of the fundamental problems of comparative urban political inquiry. Variability in units of analysis, which stems from variation in the openness of city politics, is over-come by taking as the focus of inquiry the network of organ-isations which converge on the local territorial area. Analysis proceeds by defining a focal organisation and analysing how it manages its various dependences in the service of defending or expanding its domain. Comparative inquiry then involves investigation of the characteristics of focal organisations, their networks and the environment (or context) of the latter, as well as the manner in which these factors shape the relationships of focal organisations, particularly those con-cerned with managing dependence. The concepts that arise in trying to understand the pattern of relations between organ-isations provide stability in the units of inquiry and thus help encompass such empirical variations as the size of networks and their components.

The preceding remarks also indicate how the problems of characterising the relationships between local units and those 'outside' and conceptualising the activities of non-local citizens are met. In the process of defining the units for comparative inquiry we have been analysing the types of linkages between the organisations and the strategies which involve citizen actors. Principal points here are the modes by which the focal organisation manages its dependence and the extent to which both local and non-local citizen actors are important in such efforts. The theoretical approaches built on community power analysis, systems theory, 'localism' and spatial allocations do not adequately address these problems. In general, the conceptual tools provided by an interorganisational focus allow us to take account of the most salient features of city politics, particularly variation in patterns of governance and the openness of local arenas. In Norton Long's term,[55] the city is 'unwalled' and the complexities implied by this observation must be the starting-point of our theorising about comparative urban politics.

[55]   Norton Long, *The Unwalled City* (New York: Basic Books, 1972).

Urban Politics: An Overview

Ken Young

To attempt an all-encompassing review of problems and prospects within the field of urban politics would be to exceed the bounds of my own competence, and to trespass upon that of my co-contributors. I propose instead to touch upon a limited number of issues which arise from these seven essays and which relate to urban political research as presently carried out in Britain. I direct my remarks in the main to a number of key issues in the study of *political values,* one of the all-pervasive themes in this field. I go on from there to set out some brief observations on research strategies. But we need first to face the question of why we study urban politics at all.

WHY AN 'URBAN' POLITICS?

Many readers, and perhaps many more potential readers, will have found cause to quarrel with our title. What is distinctively *urban*, rather than merely *local,* in the phenomena which each of us, in the course of our professional activities, has chosen to study? A ready answer is to reply that we have been concerned with politics *in cities,* for simple reasons of situational convenience. Most British universities are located in the areas of greatest economic activity and urban agglomeration: in so far as university researchers engage in community studies, they encounter city halls, ghettos, commuter suburbs, working-class streets, areas of planning blight, 'gin and Jaguar' belts, and public housing estates. However, while situationalism is an explanation of the past growth of urban analysis, it is not viable as a justification for our current focus upon urbanism (or urbanity) as distinct from locality.

(i) The prevalence of urbanisation

It has been calculated that by 1960 no less than a third of the world's population was living in large urban places; the rate of change to the end of the twentieth century is likely to produce a result where 'the average distribution as between the city and the country will roughly correspond with the situation existing in Britain alone around the middle of the nineteenth century, when half the population could be described as urban'.[1] If the prediction and the analogy hold, we may expect questions of urban form and containment, administration and finance, crime, movement, housing and welfare services to occupy the same place in the political arena as has been the case in Britain since the mid-Victorian period. Such questions are and will continue to be inescapable even under apolitical and anti-political regimes. The politics of urban issues, that is, issues which arise from and relate to urban populations, will be pervasive enough to demand our attention in the future as they have in the past.

(ii) Concentrations of power

There are also features of politics in cities which are not to be found in less densely populated areas. For the political scientists one of the leading features of cities is the organisation and scale of political activity arising, as Stanyer's paper suggests, from the loss of a face-to-face politics. Wirth's classic formulations on the nature of urbanism have of course been subject to extensive reappraisal over the past two decades, as Williams notes, but in this respect at least they stand the test of empirical inquiry. The politics of cities is the politics of political machines, of organisations which do not depend for their efficacy upon personal knowledge, day-to-day contact between actors, or the social sanctions which in smaller communities serve to structure voting behaviour and other forms of political activity.

In consequence, politics in British cities is more closed than is the case in the market towns and counties of the British Isles.[2] And as we are now aware, city politics is also

---

1   H. J. Dyos, *Urbanity and Suburbanity*, Inaugural Lecture (Leicester: Leicester Univ. Press, 1973) p. 9. Dyos's figures are from the calculations of Kingsley Davis.

2   One example of a 'closed' urban authority is described in Ruth Butterworth, 'Islington Borough Council: Some Characteristics of Single Party Rule', *Politics*, May 1966, pp. 21-31. Butterworth highlights the interaction between family connection and control of the party which produced a 'tribalised' ruling Labour group.

more highly stratified than even common-sense models of power and partisanship would suggest.[3] Here is one more respect in which we may follow Peter Hall's analysis and suggest that the British (or indeed the European) city is more fully an expression of *urban* culture than the North American.[4] The features of closedness, stratification, electoral passivity and low-profile government, when added to massive concentrations of Labour voters in urban centres, have on occasions given rise to the distinctively autocratic style of city regime which enabled a past Labour Prime Minister to refer to the ruling group on the late London County Council as 'the nearest thing to a totalitarian state in Western Europe'.[5] These concentrations of power and their consequences lend their own distinctiveness to the field of urban political analysis.

(iii) Spatial structure and social structure

Williams has argued, both in this volume and elsewhere, that the spatial organisation of cities is the key variable in explaining the allocation of certain types of resources. The actual distribution of populations results in differential allocations of 'real income'. These differences, arising in part from 'spillover' effects, are compounded by patterns of land tenure. Spatial locations may then be regarded as goods of varying values. These goods are allocated in part by market forces, and in part authoritatively through the operation of public power. Elkin's critique of Williams is an attack on this 'essentialist' conception of urban politics, for he argues that the allocation of urban space does not differ significantly from allocations of other types of value. I feel this to be an overstatement: space is not *just* a value allocated by the govermental/market nexus, but also has the characteristics of

[3] Ian Budge, J. A. Brand, Michael Margolis and A. L. M. Smith, *Political Stratification and Democracy* (London: Macmillan, 1972).

[4] This argument is fully developed in an important but rarely cited essay by Hall on 'The Urban and the Suburban Culture', in Richard Eells and Clarence Walton (eds.), *Man in the City of the Future* (Toronto: Collier-Macmillan, 1968).

[5] Quoted in Ken Young, 'Political Party Organisation', in Gerald Rhodes (ed.), *The New Government of London: The First Five Years* (London: Weidenfeld & Nicolson, 1972).

a power resource. As such, spatial allocations feed back into the urban political process in a more direct and immediate manner than do other goods distributed by the urban system. The special quality of the relationship between location and power in the urban setting therefore adds further significance to the politics of cities.

(iv) Micro-democracy

Finally, I would argue that it is only in the urban system that the great issues of politics under mass suffrage are fought out. The extensions of the franchise in 1867 and 1884 were seen by many Conservatives as threatening both traditional individual freedoms and the existing distribution of wealth. In the years which followed the publication of the *Radical Manifesto* the 'condition of the people' threatened or promised to become the central issue of British politics. That potential was not fully realised.[6] It was only at the local level that the issues of redistribution, of socialism and anti-socialism, and of the relation between the individual and authority have come alive. Inter-class conflict, inter-group conflict and the 'man *vs.* state' conflict may all be observed in the course of urban transition, as for example when 'the blacks, the bulldozer and the bourgeoisie' threaten a long-established working-class community. Whether those conflicts are latent or manifest they encapsulate far more of the fundamentals of politics than the matters which are the exclusive preserve of Westminster, Whitehall and Fleet Street.

These arguments as to the pervasiveness, distinctiveness and significance of urban politics serve in my view to delineate a discrete field of inquiry. The structure of the field is well indicated by the several contributors, although much of what they discuss has a wider applicability than the merely urban locale, and many of their suggestions are pertinent to the study of local-level politics outside the cities.

It is beyond dispute that political scientists must develop interdisciplinary skills if they are to provide tenable explanations of the processes and effects of urban power

[6]   Harold J. Schultz (ed.), *English Liberalism and the State: Individualism or Collectivism?* (Lexington, Mass.: D. C. Heath, 1972).

structures. What, however, should be their order of priority? My own reading of the preceding essays suggests to me that certain aspects of the study of political values may be identified as being an underdeveloped interdisciplinary area of paramount importance for explanation.

VALUES IN THE URBAN POLITICAL SYSTEM

Several contributors have touched directly or obliquely upon the question of values, although the meanings they attribute to this elusive term are not altogether congruent with one another. In some circumstances, the political analyst views value as 'a desired event — a goal event. That x values y means that x acts so as to bring about the consummation of y. The act of valuing we call "valuation", and we speak of the object or situation desired as value.'[7] It is this meaning which some of us have used when speaking in Eastonian terms of 'the authoritative allocation of values'. There are well-known problems in operationalising for research purposes such a value formulation. One problem lies in the assignment of weights to values. Another lies in the difficulties of predicting how values may be traded off against one another. The possibility of trade-offs inclines some researchers to view a multitude of values as reducible to a utility function.[8]

To use the term 'value' in this one-dimensional sense seems to me to be unduly restricting. Common usage indicates the multi-dimensionality of value; any thorough analysis of the term must reflect this multi-dimensionality by distinguishing a number of legitimate and comprehensible usages. In one of the few attempts to clarify the issues in value research, Jacob and Flink chose to identify as 'values' 'only the normative standards by which human beings are influenced in their choice among the alternative courses of action which they

[7] Harold Lasswell and Abraham Kaplan, *Power and Society* (New Haven: Yale Univ. Press, 1950) p. 16.
[8] I am grateful to Ann Richardson of Goldsmiths' College, London, for drawing my attention to this possibility, although I remain unconvinced as to the substitutability of the differing dimensions of value.

perceive'.[9] This formulation, although probably closer to common British usage than values-as-goal-events, is nevertheless similarly restricting. It is clear that many broader values at a world-view level are important for political analysis; we might therefore prefer to follow Angell in defining values as 'lasting preferences for the way in which one's social world is structured and operated'.[10]

My own inclination is instead to conceive of values in the wider and more diverse manner outlined by Kluckhohn, who has been associated with perhaps the most fruitful body of value research outside the sphere of political science.[11] As Kluckhohn argues:

> Existence and value are intimately related, interdependent, and yet — at least at the analytic level — conceptually distinct. It is a fact of both introspection and observation that there are three fundamental types of experiencing: what is or is believed (existential); what I and/or other want (desire(d)); and what I and/or other ought to want (the desirable).[12]

If 'the desirable' is considered to include behavioural norms as well as volitional norms, then we have here in Kluckhohn's formulation a versatile and sensitive concept of value. At least on superficial inspection, it embraces world-views, response styles, goals, standards of judgement and the several

[9]   Philip E. Jacob and James J. Flink, *Values and their Function in Decision-making*, a special supplement to the *American Behavioural Scientist*, May 1962.
[10] Alan Angell, quoted ibid., p. 20.
[11] The names of Clyde and Florence Kluckhohn are inseparable from the activity of value research. The most comprehensive exploration of values is probably the study of five communities published by Florence Kluckhohn and Fred L. Strodtbeck (with the assistance, among others, of Clyde Kluckhohn) as *Variations in Value Orientations* (Evanston, Ill.: Row, Peterson, 1961). There is little evidence that this important body of work has had any impact upon political science. To my knowledge, only one penetrating study of political values has been carried out: see International Studies of Values in Politics, *Values and the Active Community* (New York: Free Press, 1971).
[12] Clyde Kluckhohn, quoted in Jacob and Flink, *Values and their Function*, p. 11. Jacob and Flink in fact chose not to follow Kluckhohn's conception of value, but to narrow down the term's range of meaning.

residual dimensions of value as used by some of the contributors to this volume.

A rigorous exploration of politically salient values would go on from this point to establish a taxonomy of values and a set of postulates about the causal significance of particular values for a range of specified decision areas. The constraints of space, alas, allow neither of these lines of inquiry to be pursued here. The one point that I would make in passing is that the values touched upon in the several essays presented here related for the most part to *personal* service delivery. An area of far greater neglect is the systematic study of values relating to *environmental* policy. [13]

I propose now to bring forward three key concepts within the field of urban political analysis, all of which have significant value content. These three areas are urban imagery, localism, and professionalism.

(i) Urban imagery

The concept of the urban image exemplifies Kluckhohn's interdependence of existence and value. Unfortunately it is seemingly unknown in political research. The socio-spatial work best known to political scientists is that concerned with describing the 'objective' urban structure, and is unremittingly positivistic. [14] Only in very recent years has confidence in these techniques of social area analysis begun to wilt under accusations of mere data 'gigantism' and the more explicitly phenomenological critiques of the perceptual geographers. [15]

[13] Some interesting preliminary work by Richard Batley is reported in 'An Explanation of Non-participation in Planning', *Policy and Politics,* Dec 1972, pp. 95-114.

[14] The most recent and daunting example of this work is Brian Berry (ed.), *City Classification Handbook: Methods and Applications* (New York: Wiley, 1972).

[15] For two general reviews of the more phenomenoligical approaches, see R. J. Johnston, 'Mental Maps: An Assessment', in John Rees and Peter Newby (eds.), *Behavioural Perspectives in Geography* (London: Middlesex Polytechnic, 1973); Brian Goodey, *Perception of the Environment: An Introduction to the Literature,* Occasional Paper No. 17 (Univ. of Birmingham Centre for Urban and Regional Studies, 1971). The pioneering methodological work was K. Lynch, *The Image of the City* (Cambridge, Mass.: M.I.T. Press, 1960). A more general treatment is Anselm Strauss, *Images of the American City* (New York: Free Press, 1961).

But there are no signs yet of a corresponding reorientation among political scientists. On the contrary, the utility of social area analysis techniques in aiding research on patterns of voting behaviour by defining the spatial distribution of social groups is only now coming to be fully appreciated.

The question of how such spatial distributions are *perceived* by elite and mass actors has yet to be explored by political scientists, a surprising fact in the light of the influence that such perceptions may have upon political action. Among the politically interesting aspects are the relationships between urban structure and urban perceptions, and the incongruent images that different political actors have of the same 'objective' reality. Perhaps only professional planners and a handful of lay policy-makers ever envision all the elements of a city's area. For the rest, as Anselm Strauss puts it, 'the various kinds of urban perceptions held by the residents of a city are constructed from spatial representations resulting from membership in particular social worlds'.[16] We know little of those worlds or of the many representations of the city constructed therein. Such explorations in urban imagery as have been carried out to date have dealt in the main with mass populations, or such special sub-groups as school and university students.[17] To a very small degree, 'mental mapping' as an aid to policy-making has been carried out in a number of cities.[18] But we have yet to begin an attempt to discover the perceptual maps of the policy-makers themselves, an area which may be crucial for the explanation of those decisions which help shape the urban environment.

Perceptions are inseparable from values, for the way in which the physical and social environment is perceived directly affects residential preferences. Such preferences may well have a political impact, as when residential qualities are seen as being threatened; the earlier work of Williams im-

---

16 Strauss, ibid., p. 67.
17 For a report of some of this work, see especially Peter Gould and Rodney White, *Mental Maps* (Harmondsworth: Penguin Books, 1974).
18 Brian Goodey, 'Regional and Urban Images in Decision-making and Planning', in Rees and Newby (eds.), *Behavioural Perspectives in Geography*.

mediately springs to mind. Both values and perceptions are also present in preferences for alternative patterns of urban governmental structure. I would hypothesise at this point a connection between elite images of urban diversity and preferences for decentralised governmental structures on the one hand, and elite images of urban unity and preferences for centralised governmental structure on the other. My present research at Canterbury is concerned in part with testing this hypothesis.

Urban imagery may then eventually prove to be a powerful tool in the explanation of land-use policies, in the explanation of patterns of intergovernmental relations, and in the explanation of the social forces that underpin alternative structures of government. It is in respect of these latter questions that urban images of diversity are frequently given expression in the familiar and potent rhetoric of localism.

(ii) Localism

The existence of local government and its survival (albeit in modified form) in the face of managerialist-rationalist ideologies of efficiency, effectiveness, and economy is testimony to the strength of the societal values embodied in autonomous local institutions. 'Localism' – the emotive symbolisation of the values of the small place – affects the structuring of institutions through its demands for two-tier government in the great conurbations and in the rural counties. It also pervades intergovernmental relations and underlies the distaste for partisanship in local affairs.

'The values of local democracy' in so far as they justify the *existence* of local government are an aspect of localism that has been covered at length by other writers, most recently Sharpe.[19] In contrast, the extent to which particular structures of urban government are the institutionalised expression of particular belief-systems is an unexplored question, but there are strong indications that support for decentralised urban government is associated with a positive evaluation of diversity, community, intimacy and responsiveness – all of

[19] L. J. Sharpe, 'Theories and Values of Local Government', *Political Studies*, June 1970, pp. 153-74.

them strongly localist values — while support for strong area-wide single-tier urban government is associated with a positive evaluation of efficiency, equity, orderliness and potency — generally anti-localist values.[20]

Localism is also manifested in intergovernmental relations, both in the horizontal (or inter-area) and in the vertical (or inter-tier) planes. Intergovernmental relations have enjoyed a certain amount of attention from researchers in the past, but only recently have we seen a burgeoning of interest linked to the development of suitable analytic tools for their analysis. This new phase of intergovernmental studies is reflected in Elkin's essay, where the 'openness' of city politics demands that we make use of interorganisation theory; it is reflected also in the movement to transcend corporate planning and explore the 'intercorporate dimension' of government;[21] and in the appointment by Birmingham University's Institute of Local Government Studies (the mysterious INLOGOV referred to elsewhere in this volume) of a specialist Lecturer in Inter-Authority Relations (a post in respect of which the Institute may wisely abandon their passion for mnemonics). The studies which will be generated by such developments may be expected to throw new light on this aspect of localism.

A third manifestation of the forces of localism is to be found in the widespread persistence of anti-partisan sentiments within local government. There is plenty of evidence — some of it cited here by Stanyer — of a widespread emotive distaste for 'party politics in local government'. Clearly, the intervention of nationally oriented or controlled parties in local elections and into the policy processes of local authorities may well have a 'delocalising' effect, both in so far as local actions or declarations may occur with a view to their

[20] Support for localism seems to be strongest among Conservatives and support for centralism strongest among Radicals. I have touched upon the Conservative support for localist solutions to the problems of metropolitan governmental structure in 'The Politics of London Government, 1880-1899', *Public Administration*, Spring 1973, pp. 91-108, and in 'The Conservative strategy for London since 1855,' *The London Journal*, Spring 1975.

[21] J. Friend, J. M. Power and C. J. L. Yewlett, *Public Planning: The Intercorporate Dimension* (London: Tavistock, 1974).

national impact, and in so far as the formal sphere of local autonomy may be eroded by these non-governmental local — national linkages. As Stanyer suggested, recent changes in British local government are likely to increase partisanship; they also provide an opportunity to observe the resistance to it, thereby bringing to the surface the often unstated values of localism.[22]

(iii) Professionalism

Several of the authors raised the question of the significance and influence of professionals in local policy-making. If future research is to follow the leads which they have given and focus upon the role of the professionals, it may be helpful to point out at this stage some problems in the relationship between professional values and professional behaviour.

An obvious defining characteristic of professionals is that they *profess*. In Everett Hughes' words:

> They profess to know better than others the nature of certain matters, and to know better than their clients what ails them or their affairs. This is the essence of the professional idea and the professional claim. From it flow many consequences. The professionals claim the exclusive right . . . to give the kind of advice derived from their special lines of knowledge.[23]

Other writers have stressed the autonomy of professional workers and the primacy of their orientation towards 'the profession', which is the sole arbiter of standards and the sole legitimate source of control, as well as to the strength of the bond which exists between the professional man and his client.[24]

How then do professionals operate in the context of such

[22] Anti-partisan localism is stronger among Conservative voters: I discuss the ambivalence of the Conservative Party on the question of partisan local elections in my forthcoming *Local politics and the rise of Party* (Leicester: Univ. Press, 1975).

[23] Everett Hughes, 'Professions', *Daedalus*, Fall 1963, pp. 655-68.

[24] See generally the special issue of *Daedalus*, ibid.; Amitai Etzioni (ed.), *The Semi-Professions and their Organisation: Teachers, Nurses, Social Workers* (New York: Free Press, 1969); Terence Johnson, *Professions and Power* (London: Macmillan, 1972).

organisations as local governments? In the first place, the professional is caught in a tension between two foci of authority, towards the profession and towards the employer. The contradiction is commonly resolved by the development of specialist associations exclusively for public service professionals (thus de-emphasising the rigours of the external claim) and by authorities developing patterns of organisation, procedure and practice which reconcile the need for superordinate control on the employer's part with the need for a colleague control pattern of authority on the part of the professional worker. The effect of these two factors is to breed a special kind of hybrid animal, the 'professional-administrator'. Deprived of the traditional professional freedom to choose his paymaster, the professional-administrator can at least choose his *problem*, retaining thereby much initiative in his own hands, and compensating for (or even subverting) the formal pattern of superordinate lay control.[25]

It would nevertheless be wrong to suggest that the implicit tensions in the role of 'professional-administrator' are thereby entirely resolved. Problems arise from the bond of obligation between the professional worker and his client, and do not affect all professions equally. The City Engineer's or Chief Architect's life is simplified by the fact that his employer *is also his client*. Not so fortunate is the Director of Social Services who is faced with the employer and the recipient, both of whom articulate claims to his primary ('client') responsibility. The hybrid professional-administrator in charge of social services (who is often troubled by doubts as to his professional legitimacy) can resolve the conflict by a reaffirmation of his loyalty to the employer. Yet in doing so he may well distance himself from his field staff, who neither possess nor need to possess his hybrid qualities, and whose primary loyalty in conflict situations may lie with the recipient rather than the employer. The question becomes one of 'whose values should prevail?' The organisation-based 'semi-professional' social worker cannot answer

---

[25]   These speculations arise in part from Bernard Barber's stimulating discussion of 'Some Problems in the Sociology of the Professions', in *Daedalus*, ibid.

the question with confidence; the urban planner is only now beginning to ask it.

The second range of problems in professional values is less apparent. It is clear that status hierarchies exist between layment and professionals within professions, between professions, and sometimes between the 'semi-professions' and their professional reference groups. It is also probable that professions may be ranked on a 'hard — soft' continuum, from the engineers who possess 'a trained incapacity to deal with human affairs' to the personal service professions whose trained capacity so to deal is the essence of their claim to professional status.[26] Are some professions 'more professional' than others? What are the determinants of professional distance? The answers to these questions would tell us much about the structuring of power relations within the urban governmental organisation, both in terms of relations between groups of serving professionals, and in terms of relations between serving professionals and lay members who happen to be members of professions themselves. The urban political analyst does not have to look far in social science literature to gain insight into these questions of professional values and behaviour.

A RESEARCH STRATEGY RESTATED

This concluding essay has attempted briefly to justify our interest in urban politics as a field of inquiry, and to select a small number of concepts among those dimensions of value which seem most salient in the urban political scene. The selection is a necessarily arbitrary one and for the most part is intended simply to complement the many important points raised by the other contributors. In making that selection I was reminded of the maxims stated a few years ago by Anselm Strauss. Strauss's advice has gone largely unheeded in this country, and therefore bears restatement. It was: *study the unstudied, study the unusual, minimise ideological*

---

[26] For a discussion of the 'personal service professions', see Paul Halmos, *The Faith of the Counsellors* (London: Constable, 1965), and the same author's *The Personal Service Society* (London: Constable, 1970).

commitment, and *study comparatively.*[27] The last of these
four maxims needs no further elaboration here in view of the
ground already covered by the other contributors. The other
three seem, however, to be worth repetition in the specific
context of British urban political research, which has suffered
in the past from some misdirection.

We may take *study the unusual* as an exhortation to look
closely at out-of-pattern occurrences: a high incidence of
deviance in an area of favourable social conditions; high welfare expenditure in a Conservative-dominated leafy commuter suburb; the opening-up in one locality of the local
decision-making process to the entire population; persistent
patterns of non-partisan voting in a highly urbanised area.
The possible examples are endless and any of us could name a
number of them.[28]

The utility of the maxim *study the unstudied* strikes one
forcibly in any consideration of the opportunity cost of
specific research projects. Much work has been done, for
example, on social mix and social relations in planned New
Towns; yet we have a greater need to know about such topics
as client and community perceptions of social work services,
where such research as has been carried out resulted in more
substantial increments to our understanding of urban life.[29]

Alternatively, we may take 'the unstudied' to refer to areas

[27] Anselm Strauss, 'Strategies for Discovering Urban Theory', in Leo
Schnore and Henry Fagin (eds.), *Urban Research and Policy Planning* (Beverly Hills, Calif.: Sage Publications, 1967).

[28] Two good examples of the study of the unusual are Wyn Grant,
'Non-partisanship in British Local Politics', *Policy and Politics*, Mar
1973, pp. 241-54.
and William Hampton and Penelope Pike, 'The Open Council and
Public Participation: The Leichardt Experience', *Policy and
Politics*, Sep 1974, pp. 37-50.

[29] Among the examples of universal phenomena which are rarely
studied are those reported in John E. Mayer and Noel Timms, *The
Client Speaks: Working Class Impressions of Casework* (London:
Routledge & Kegan Paul, 1970); and in B. Glastonbury, M. Burdett
and R. Austin, 'Community Perceptions and the personal Social
Services', *Policy and Politics*, Mar 1973, pp. 191-212. The recent
and valuable fashion for 'oral history' is testimony to a new
strategy of 'compensatory research into the unstudied' among
contemporary historians.

which by convention are simply not researched or to questions which are customarily not asked. Certain policy-related questions may be deemed improper, not just by those in the field of action (subject resistance is common and understandable), but also by others in academic life. The researcher who formulates a hypothesis that students may benefit from studying at an institution of higher education near their homes and remaining domiciled at home, or a hypothesis that in certain respects comprehensive education, unstreamed classes or progressive teaching methods may have specific detrimental consequences, can sometimes face the censure of his colleagues. Other more general issues — 'working-class authoritarianism' for example — seem to be similarly sensitive. A strategy of compensatory research is needed to ensure that unfashionable questions are not neglected.

This point leads to the third injunction to *minimise indeological commitment*. This seems at the present time a desperately unfashionable maxim, although when Strauss exemplifies his point by warning researchers away from current public policy issues he may well win applause from the ideologically committed — if perhaps for the wrong reasons. Many social scientists in Britain belong to the liberal (and some to the illiberal) left; their ideological commitment may result in a biasing effect upon the total product of research activity.

The problem is not primarily one of ideological entrapment within the research situation, nor is it one of falsifying evidence; it is one that arises from the earlier stage of framing research questions. The individual committed researcher may well frame his or her personal research priorities in an unexceptional manner, but the aggregate and cumulative effect of many such unrelated personal research decisions as to what is interesting and what is not may be to bias our understanding of society profoundly.[30]

---

[30] Consider, for example, the massive imbalance in the literatures of socialist and anti-socialist history respectively. I am reminded of a late colleague who, when told that I was currently researching the Conservative Party, replied 'How boring!', a remark that seems as significant of a broad tendency as of a personal lack of intellectual curiosity.

A further point about active political commitment may also be mentioned. The politically engaged researcher may well suffer from discrimination in data access, to either documentary sources or to opportunities for observation. Access to local Labour politicians (and even to the private caucus meetings and records of Labour groups) may be gained through the personal contacts which arise from activism; comparable access may be denied by the opposing party.[31] Engagement would not be a problem for data access if academic researchers were approximately evenly divided in their political leanings, but this seems not to be the case. It would matter less were British urban government customarily more open, less secretive; unfortunately it is not, and the researcher has to both win and to *merit* trust.

We cannot be expected to revise our ideological allegiances; but individual researchers and research-funding agencies can consciously strive for greater balance, greater detachment and a strategy of compensatory research.

CONCLUSION

The essays which comprise this collection reveal a wide range of interests on the part of the contributors. They do not encompass the entire range of questions within the field of urban politics, and we would not claim that they do so. Nor is the range of understanding which they offer confined exclusively to the urban setting. But in accepting the need for such a symposium each of the participants implicitly concurred in the need for theory-building. We each wish to

---

[31] A good example of a committed research worker being accorded differential access is recorded in Enid Wistrich, *Local Government Reorganisation: The First Years of Camden* (London: London Borough of Camden, 1972). Wistrich writes:

> The Labour Group of Camden Council made available the minutes of the Group's meetings and of its Policy Committee and I was also able to see the proceedings of the (Labour) Camden Local Government Committee. Although the Conservatives did not feel able to let a political opponent read the minutes of their Joint Liaison Committee, Mr W. Jay, agent of the Hampstead Conservative Association, told me a great deal about its scope and about the Conservative political organisation in Camden . . .

transcend *ad hoc* partial explanations; we each wish to avoid a decline into our anecdotage. Hopefully, by following the leads given here as to substantive questions, research strategies and disciplinary eclecticism, we may yet begin to construct the urban political theory which is our common aim.

Index

local government, *cont.*
  scope, 70-1
  status, 126-7
  'two tier' systems, 44
  'localism', 193-5
local-level politics, 166-7
locational politics, 167-71
Lodz, 158
London, 54, 112, 124, 133, 141
  County Council (LCC), 187
  Greater London Council (GLC), 141
  local government legislation (1974), 43-51
Long, N., 184
Loveridge, R., 67-8
Lowi, T. J., 6n, 19n, 21
Lucking, R. C., *et al.*, 60n
Lynch, K., 191n

Macey, J., 121n
McKenzie, R. T., and Silver, A., 76n
Madrid, 117
Manchester, 35
Mangin, W., 119n
March, J., and Simon, H., 172n
Marriott, O., 121n
Mayer, J. E., 97n
  and Timms, N., 198n
'megalopolis', 136
metropolitan reform, 138-41
Meyerson, M., and Banfield, E. C., 169n
Miller, D. C., 10n, 12n, 163n
Miller, S., and Reisman, F., 73n
Minns, R., 94n
Mlinar, Z., and Teune, H., 168n
models, 33-5, 37-51, 69-70, 152
Mogulof, M. B., 139n
Morgenstern, O., 92n
Morris, D. S., and Newton, K., 45n
Moscow, 118
Mumford, L., 127n
municipal services, 111-12
Municipal Year Book, 35
Muth, R. F., 110n

National Health Service, 65n
Nationalist parties, 51
need, 63-4, 79, 89, 90-1, 92-104
  need-demand relationships, 102-3
  need-supply relationships, 103-4
neo-functionalism, 149-50
Netzer, D., 124n
Neumann, J. von, 92n
Newcastle-under-Lyme, 29n
New Haven, 8-9
Newton, K., 6n, 33n, 58n
New York City, 130
  Metropolitan Region, 11
North, R. C., *et al.*, 153n

Oliver, F. R., and Stanyer, J., 45n
Olsen, M., 87
'openness', 160-2, 164, 170, 171, 180, 194
'opportunities', 114-16
organisational pluralism, 20-1
organisation theory, 171-84, 194
Osborn, R. J., 117n
Ostrom, E., 140n
Ostrom, V., 140n

Packman, J., 63n, 101
panel studies, 29-30
Parenti, M., 8n
Parker, J. K., 139n
Parkin, F., 73n
partisanship, 34-5, 36-7, 40-3, 47
party systems, 74-7
Pentland, C., 143n, 144, 149
Peru, 158
Peschek, D., and Brand, J., 67n
Poland, 158
police, 129-31
Policy and Politics, xiv, 88n, 94n
political integration, 142-50
political parties (see also under specific parties), 12, 13, 15-17, 34-6, 45-51, 188
  local, 16, 35
  national instability of, 48-9
  national/local multiplier, 46-7
Polsby, N., 5